The Analogy Book of Related Words

Your Secret Shortcut to Power Writing

by Selma Glasser

Communication Creativity
425 Cedar Street • P. O. Box 909
Buena Vista, Colorado 81211

Although the author and publisher have made every effort to ensure the accuracy and completeness of information contained in this book, we assume no responsibility for errors, inaccuracies, omissions, or any inconsistency herein. Any slights of people, places, or organizations are unintentional.

Library of Congress Cataloging-in-Publication Data

Glasser, Selma
    The analogy book of related words: your secret shortcut to power writing / by Selma Glasser.
        p.   cm.
    ISBN 0-918880-23-8 (tradepbk.): $12.95
    1. Vocabulary. 2. English language—Synonyms and antonyms.
I. Title.
PE1449.G54 1990
428.1—dc20   90-32271
                                                         CIP

DEDICATION
and
ACKNOWLEDGMENTS

It is fitting that *The Analogy Book of Related Words* be dedicated to my late husband, Allen, who originally wrote of this technique for *Contest* Magazine. Mrs. Lillie Wehe of San Antonio, Texas suggested the basic idea of putting it into book form, which led to its ultimate development. I would like to acknowledge that my articles, contest entries, verses, and other books have been enhanced by the utilization of analogy.

The *Glasser Guide to Filler Writing,* a mail order course—which is also taught at colleges from New York to California—incorporates some of the teachings found in *The Analogy Book of Related Words.*

Further, this volume is dedicated to readers and writers who have used this technique and reported the many writing successes it has brought them. And, especially, my thanks goes to the publisher, without whose faith in the book, it could not have been accomplished.

FOREWORD

The Analogy Book of Related Words is a unique "wordstorming" partner. A one-of-a-kind reference, it's an invaluable aid for all who seek to create powerful prose. This key word formula can be adapted for any form of writing or speaking. It serves as a dynamic idea generator, practically coaxing the words onto pages.

Just as the computer is revolutionizing the way writers approach their craft, this book offers a unique formula for success. The secret weapon revealed here belongs in the arsenal of every writer and public speaker.

Freelancers, novelists, educators, speakers, trainers, ministers, entertainers, public officials, any intellectual—will find this anthology of terms and examples refreshing and useful. It shows how to add pizzazz to the written and spoken word.

It is invaluable for those who originate advertising copy or are charged with composing convincingly written promotional material. Copywriters can employ this to give their work added zest, style, and momentum.

Savvy contesters long ago discovered using this system allows them to outfox and outflank the competition—and capture top prizes. Within these pages they'll find fresh idea starters and illustrated examples to spur their creativity.

Another way to use this book is as a party game. On a chilly winter evening, see who can create the longest list of related words. It can even be played as a form of Solitaire! Pick a subject and challenge yourself to develop a string of associated terms—or use our lists to spawn a story. And writing instructors can build exercises in creativity around *The Anthology Book of Related Words*.

But this isn't just theory. Author Selma Glasser has been practicing what she preaches for 20 years. She has seen five of her books published, written scores of articles and columns, and is considered the guru of contesting—with an enormous number of prizes to her credit. We're proud to present Selma's proven formula. Applied wisely, it will help you have more fun, enjoy new prominence, and reap greater profits.

Marilyn Ross
Publisher

TABLE OF CONTENTS

INTRODUCTION

What is an analogy? Simply defined, it is the description of your subject in terms borrowed from an entirely different field. Here's an example: "Analog is the *thread* of interest *woven* into the *fabric* of any form of writing. It's up to the enterprising wordsmith to *spin* some into the *tapestry* of his or her writing." Similar terms can be adapted to describe the virtues of almost any product or idea.

This book was conceived for people who enter and win creative write-in contests. The formula's highly acclaimed success in all fields of writing, however, has proven that this technique is an invaluable tool for coaxing words onto paper. Hence not only contestants, but also ad copywriters—authors—educators—speakers—entertainers—even presidents employ this device in their writings, routines, and lectures.

Said former President Reagan in a speech intended to set the stage for his final act of the presidency, "When you come to town, *open big*. And, well, now it's time for an even bigger finish and a good *curtain call*."

While best adapted for description, analogy can also be profitably employed for slogans and jingles, headlines and captions, verses and articles. Highly paid copywriters often employ this technique. An American Airlines headline reads *Paint* San Juan *red* for very little *green*. Here's how the Beverly Wilshire sloganizes about itself: A *jewel* in a *perfect setting*. A support swim trunk ad proclaims you can Hide your *spare tire* in our *trunk*. A Campbell soup ad reads How to *travel first class* on *economy fare*.

Clever epigrams frequently contain analogies. For instance, "Elbow grease is the best lubricant for those rusty mental gears" or "Marriage is like a violin. After the music is over, the strings are still attached."

Prominent authors often interlace their fiction with analogies. In *Of Human Bondage*, W. Somerset Maugham writes, "For a year he had *swum* in a *sea* of darkness. Fortunately he had reached *calm waters* at last." In *Miss Lonelyhearts* Nathanael West suggests sad letters are "*stamped* from the *dough* of suffering with a heartshaped *cookie cutter*."

My own review of the delightful comedy show, "Angry Housewives," went like this: "The *percolating* plot starts on a *low burner* but *boils over* with *bubbling* talent, show-stopping songs and intoxicating humor. It's a *well done* show *cooking* with *gags*." (It never hurts to insert a pun or parody.)

Using a postal analog, here's an epigram I sold to *Family Weekly*. It was later reprinted in *Reader's Digest*: "Remarks that are *uncalled* for are usually *delivered*." You can sell *Playboy* with analogy, too. How about, "Our unabashed dictionary defines *alimony* as dis*interest compounded annually*" (from banking terms). And how about this fire analogy: "A guy with *money* to *burn* usually meets his *match*."

Witty quips are entertaining not only in planned presentations, but also in impromptu conversation. At a Republican rally the banter included "Let's *plant* a *Bush* in the White House!" Joan Rivers asked an attractive guest how she managed to stay in shape. The glamorous actress answered that it was simply good maintenance—to which Joan retorted she hadn't found a good mechanic yet.

Are you beginning to appreciate the quality and value of this formula? These illustrations point out how the technique of analogy is a popular, prize-winning, and creative professional tool when applied skillfully and appropriately.

To be effective, this device should be used sparingly. In a slogan or short paragraph, three or four well-chosen related words are usually sufficient. Using too many may cause readers or listeners to pay more attention to your cleverness than to your message. Never make your method too obvious; it should be deft, not pretentious.

Because of its nature, this collection of analogs could start anywhere and proceed with random subjects. But to systematize the material for instant, easy reference, I've listed the basic themes in a dictionary format: from A to Z—Acting to Zodiac. And there is a handy index that cross-references key words, thus helping you locate appropriate terms.

Each category has been refined using logic and common sense. While technically spiders are arachnids, many people think of them as insects—so they're included in the "Insect" list. And under "Animals" most amphibians, reptiles, and some mammals have been omitted. Lists alone, however, are only partially helpful. I've taken the concept further by supplying you with examples, phrases, illustrations, and humorous quips to stimulate your thinking.

Properly used, *The Anthology Book of Related Words* will be of incalculable value to any writer. Merely reading it will serve little purpose; you must apply the given material to profit from it. Even the illustrations offered are intended only to spur your creative juices.

These are stepping stones—but you must pave your own pathway to success. In composing your own analogies, better not follow the models too closely. Once published they are sure to be copied. So start planting some analogs in your work to boost your sales and win more prizes.

ACTING

acclaim
acrobat
act
acting
actor
actress
all-star
applaud
applause
audience
audition
backstage
balcony
big-time
billing
bit player
blackout
boo
book
bow
box
box office
bright lights
Broadway
burlesque
cast
character
chorus
circuit
climax
co-star
comedy
comic
concert

costume
critic
cue
curtain
debut
denouement
dialogue
director
double feature
drama
dramatic
dramatist
Emmy
emote
emotion
enact
encore
entertain
entertainment
entrance
exit
extra
fan mail
fan
farce
feature
film
finale
first night
flop
footlights
foyer
front row
gag

gallery
greasepaint
ham
headliner
heavy
hero
heroine
hit
impersonate
impersonator
impresario
ingenue
intermission
juvenile
lampoon
lead
leading lady
leading man
limelight
lines
long run
lyrics
M.C.
make-up
marquee
matinee
melodrama
menace
minstrel
miscue
motion picture
movies
musical
off-stage

opening
orchestra
Oscar
pan
part
pass
patter
perform
performance
performer
performing arts
picture
play
playbill
player
playwright
plot
portray
premiere
present
preview
produce
producer
production
program
project
prompter
props

punch line
puppet
rave notice
reel
register
rehearsal
rehearse
rescue
review
revival
road
role
run
satire
scenario
scene
scenery
screen
script
season
sellout
set
show business
show
showboat
showgirl
spotlight
stage fright

stage
stagehand
stand-in
star
stardom
stage-struck
stellar
stock
stooge
summer
supporting
talent
theatre
theatrical
theme
ticket
tour
tragedy
troupe
trouper
tryout
turkey
understudy
usher
variety
vaudeville
villain
wings

Acting Phrases

Academy Award . . . behind the scenes . . . bring down the house . . . eternal triangle . . . give a big hand . . . happy ending . . . master/mistress of ceremonies . . . name in lights . . . on the road . . . ring down the curtain . . . show must go on . . . standing room only . . . steal the show . . . take a bow . . . the curtain falls .

.. the curtain rises . . . the play's the thing . . . the plot thickens . . . there's no business like show business . . . three-ring circus . . . two on the aisle . . . all the world's a stage.

Entry Examples

I like (toothpaste) because . . . its smooth, fast PERFORMANCE is efficient, tasteful and refreshing—enhancing the BRIGHT LIGHTS of my sparkling smile and making it my STAR FEATURE.

I like (soup) because . . . with a great CAST of tasty ingredients, hearty CHARACTER, and STAR flavor, it always rates my family's APPLAUSE.

AERONAUTICS

above
accelerate
acceleration
ace
aerial
aeronautics
air mail
air
air lift
air force
aircraft
airline
airman
airplane
airport
airship
airworthy
aloft
altitude
apex
ascend
asteroid
astral
astronaut
astronomer
astronomy
atmosphere
atomic
automatic pilot
aviation
aviator
bailout
balloon
bank

beacon
beam
bird
birdman
black-out
blast-off
blimp
bomb
bombard
bomber
booster
cabin
cadet
capsule
cargo
carrier
catapult
ceiling
celestial
circle
climb
clipper
cloud
coach
coast
cockpit
combat
comet
conk out
constellation
deviate
dirigible
dispatcher
dive

down
downward
downwind
drift
drop
eagle
earth
earthling
eclipse
energy
engine
exhaust
explode
explore
fall
field
fire
fireball
first-class
fission
flair
flash
flight
fly
flyer
fog
forward
free fall
fuel
fuselage
galaxy
glide
glider
globe

glow
gondola
gravity
ground
hanger
head wind
heaven
height
high
hop
horizon
hover
hurl
intercept
interplanetary
jet
journey
jump
kite
land
landing
lark
launch
launching
level off
lift
liftoff
log
long-range
loop
luminosity
lunar
magnetic
maneuver
manned
mass
meteor
meteoric

Milky Way
missile
mission
momentum
monitor
moon
motor
navigate
nebula
nebulous
non-stop
nose-dive
nova
nuclear
observatory
off course
orbit
outer space
overcast
overhead
pad
panic button
parachute
payload
peak
pilot
plane
planet
planetary
plunge
polar
power
probe
projectile
prop
propel
propellant
propeller

propulsion
push-button
radar
range
refuel
relativity
rev up
revolution
revolve
rise
robot
rocket
rotate
rudder
runway
safety
satellite
seaplane
send up
shine
shoot
shooting star
shot
signal
sky
skyward
slipstream
soar
solar
solar system
solo
sound barrier
space station
spacesuit
space shuttle
space
spaceman
spaceship

span
speed
sphere
spin
sputnik
stall
star
star-gazer
stellar
steward
stewardess
stratosphere
streamlined
summit
sun
sunspot
supersonic
surface

tailspin
tail wind
takeoff
target
telescope
terminal
terrain
test pilot
thrust
thruster
tip
tourist
track
transport
travel
trip
turbine
unmanned

up
upward
vapor trail
vehicle
velocity
visibility
voyage
warhead
weightless
whirl
whiz
wide-body
wings
world
zenith
zeppelin
zoom

Aeronautical Phrases

Bird's-eye view . . . break the sound barrier . . . ceiling zero . . . center of gravity . . . coast-to-coast . . . don't push the panic button . . . down to earth . . . escape velocity . . . flight of fancy . . . fly like an eagle . . . flying blind . . . flying fool . . . flying saucer . . . fold its wings . . . forced landing . . . get off the ground . . . go into a tailspin . . . guided missile . . . happy landings . . . heavenly body . . . holding pattern . . . landing gear . . . loop-the-loop . . . off the beam . . . on the beam . . . out of this world . . . out to launch . . .

point of no return . . . speed of light . . . theory of relativity . . . 3-point landing . . . up in the air . . . wild blue yonder.

Entry Examples

I use (shoe polish) because . . . its SKY-HIGH shine gives my shoes an AIR of distinction that helps PRO-PEL my business and social progress, SPEEDING my career ever UPWARD.

I prefer a (pen) because . . . it TAKES OFF instantly, holds any SPEED, has visible FUEL supply, GLIDES along gracefully, and FLIES OVER the roughest PAD.

Slogan Samples

SKY-HIGH value at a DOWN-TO-EARTH price.

AGRICULTURAL AND RANCHING

acre
agriculture
alfalfa
arable
artificial
  insemination
arid
bale
baler
barley
barn
barnyard
beef
binder
blight
blossom
bough
bovine
branch
breed
bucolic
bud
bull
bush
bushel
castrate
cattle
chaff
chicken
chore
cistern
climate
clover
come up

consume
corn
cotton
country
cow
crop
cross
cultivate
cultivation
currant
dairy
dam
ditch
domestic
drainage
drought
equestrian
erosion
fallow
farm
farmer
feed
fence
fertile
fertilize
field
fleece
flesh
foliage
food
forage
frost
fruit
furrow

garden
germinate
graft
grain
granary
grass
graze
greenhouse
grist
ground
grow
growth
harvest
hatch
hay
hayseed
haystack
hedge
herd
hick
hide
hoe
hog
homestead
horse
hybrid
implement
irrigation
kernel
land
lawn
livestock
market
maverick

meat
milk
mill
miller
mow
mule
oats
orchard
pasture
peck
pick
pitchfork
plant
plantation
plow
plowboy
poultry
preserve
produce
raise
rake
ranch
rancher
reap
reaper

RFD
ripe
ripen
root
rural
rustic
rye
sand
sap
scarecrow
scythe
seed
sharecropper
shear
sickle
silo
sod
soil
sow
space
spade
spray
sprout
stable
stack

stalk
staple
steer
stem
sticks
stock
straw
swine
thresh
till
tractor
transplant
tree
trough
udder
vine
water
weed
wheat
windrow
wood
wool
yield
yoke

Agricultural and Ranching Phrases

As ye sow so shall ye reap . . . chicken feed . . .
coming through the rye . . . common garden variety . .
. cream of the crop . . . don't fence me in . . . down on
the farm . . . gone to seed . . . great open spaces . . .
know your oats . . . made hay while the sun shines . . .
Mother Earth . . . out where the tall corn grows . . .
raising cane . . . root hog or die . . . separate the wheat
from the chaff . . . sowing wild oats . . . staff of life . .
. the good earth.

Entry Example

I want to live in (state) because . . . I'd like to CULTIVATE a sunny disposition where I can HARVEST the FRUIT of my labors and enjoy the full FLOWER of leisurely living.

Slogan Sample

To CULTIVATE customers and REAP goodwill, RAISE quality, not prices!

ANATOMY

anatomy
ankle
arch
arm
artery
back
backbone
bald
beard
belly
birthmark
blind
blood
bodily
body
bone
brain
brawn
breast
brow
calf
cavity
cell
cheek
chest
chin
colon
cranium
cuticle
dental
digit
dimple
dissect
doctor

ear
elbow
embryo
eye
eyebrow
eyelash
eyelid
face
facial
feature
figure
finger
fingernail
fist
flesh
foot
forearm
forehead
frail
function
gland
gullet
gums
hair
hamstring
hand
head
health
healthy
heart
heartbeat
heel
height
hip

human
husky
instep
internal
jaw
joint
jugular
knee
kneecap
knuckle
larynx
lean
leg
ligament
limb
lip
liver
lung
manual
marrow
member
mind
moustache
mouth
muscle
nail
nape
navel
neck
nerve
nose
optic
optical
oral

organ
palate
palm
paralyze
pate
paunch
physical
physique
posture
pulse
pupil
rib
rump
scalp
shin
shoulder
skeleton
skin
skinny

skull
socket
sole
spinal
spine
spleen
stalwart
stomach
stout
strength
strong
teeth
tendon
thigh
thin
throat
thumb
tissue
toe

toenail
tongue
tooth
torso
trunk
vein
vertebra
vocal cord
waist
weak
weakness
weight
well-being
whiskers
windpipe
wrinkle
wrist

Anatomical Phrases

Achilles' heel . . . Adam's apple . . . bend an ear . . . body and soul . . . by the sweat of his brow . . . can't stomach it . . . chin up . . . cold feet . . . don't bite off more than you can chew . . . double chin . . . elbow grease . . . face lifting . . . facts of life . . . first aid . . . five senses . . . foot the bill . . . funny bone . . . get it off your chest . . . give a big hand . . . gray matter . . . grease my palm . . . green thumb . . . growing pains . . . in one ear and out the other . . . keep a stiff upper lip . . . knuckle down . . . lead with your chin . . . lean 'n mean . . . lip service . . . load off your chest . . . makes my mouth water . . . medicine man . . . muscle-bound . . . naked eye . . . nerves of steel . . . not a leg to stand on . . . oh, my aching back! . . . once on the lips, forever on the hips . . . pain in the neck . . . rib-tickler . . . sixth sense . . . sticks to your ribs . . . thumb a ride . . . thumbs down . . . thumbs up . . . time heals all wounds . . . time wounds all heels . . . toe the line . . . tongue in cheek . . . too much to swallow . . . turn the other cheek . . . 20-20 vision . . . vocal cords . . . win in a walk.

Entry Examples

(Oats) are my favorite breakfast food because . . . its BODY-building nourishment sticks to my RIBS—helping me to FACE the day with a SMILE and get a HEAD start with my work.

Anatomy Antics

Did you hear about the butcher who backed into the sausage machine? He got a little behind in his work.

Sign in a women's clothing store: "Does the end justify the Jeans?"

What's the definition of a girdle?
A hinder binder.

Spouse to mate: "If you don't stop biting off my head you'll have more brains in your stomach than in your head."

ANIMALS

alligator
amphibian
animal
anteater
antelope
antler
ape
armadillo
baboon
badger
band
bark
bat
bear
beast
beaver
bevy
biped
bird
bison
boar
brace
breed
bronco
brood
brute
buck
buffalo
bull
bunny
burro
burrow
butt
cage

camel
canine
cat
cattle
centaur
chameleon
cheetah
chimp
chimpanzee
chinchilla
chipmunk
circus
claw
clutch
colt
cougar
covey
cow
coyote
creature
crocodile
cross breed
cub
cur
deer
den
dinosaur
doe
dog
domestic
donkey
drive
drove
elephant

elk
equine
ermine
ewe
fawn
feline
ferret
filly
fleece
flock
fossil
fox
frog
fur
gaggle
gallop
game
gazelle
giraffe
gnaw
goat
gopher
gorilla
grizzly
ground hog
growl
grunt
guinea pig
habitat
hair
hare
herd
hibernate
hide

hippopotamus
hiss
hog
hoof
horn
horse
hound
howl
hunt
hunter
hyena
jackal
jackass
jaguar
jungle
kangaroo
kid
kitten
lair
lamb
leopard
lion
litter
lizard
llama
lynx
mammal
mammoth
mane
mare
mate
menagerie
mink
mongrel
monkey
moose
mouse
mule

mustang
muzzle
nag
nest
opossum
pachyderm
pack
panda
panther
paw
pelt
pig
platypus
polar bear
polecat
pony
pooch
porcupine
prey
pride
primate
puma
pup
puppy
purr
puss
quadruped
quill
rabbit
raccoon
ram
rat
reindeer
reptile
rhinoceros
rodent
sable
scavenger

serpent
sheep
shrew
skunk
sloth
snake
snout
sow
sphinx
spoor
squirrel
stag
stalk
stallion
steed
steer
swine
tame
team
territory
tiger
toad
tomcat
track
train
trainer
trap
trapper
trot
trunk
tusk
unicorn
vixen
walrus
warren
weasel
whale
whippet

wild	wolverine	zebra
wildcat	woodchuck	zoo
wolf	yak	

Animal Phrases

A wolf in sheep's clothing . . . animal kingdom . . . artificial insemination . . . beast of burden . . . black sheep . . . bring 'em back alive! . . . bull in a china shop . . . bum steer . . . busy as a beaver . . . crocodile tears . . . cross breeding . . . endangered species . . . get your goat . . . golden fleece . . . horse of a different color . . . laughing hyena . . . leopard can't change his spots . . . Noah's Ark . . . play 'possum . . . pussy-foot . . . road hog . . . sacred cow . . . shaggy dog story . . . snake in the grass . . . toss the bull by the horns . . . throw the bull . . . of Borneo . . . you can't teach an old dog new tricks.

Entry Example

I prefer (shoes) because . . . they're tough as a RHINOCEROS yet light as a GAZELLE, they BEAR up under heavy usage to earn my SEAL of satisfaction.

ART

abstract
accent
acrylic
airbrush
art
artist
artistic
artwork
atmosphere
atmospheric
background
batik
beauty
blend
bronze
brush
bust
calligraphic
calligraphy
canvas
caricature
cartoon
carve
carving
casein
cast
chalk
charcoal
chisel
clay
collage
color
color wheel
complementary

color
compose
composition
contour
contrast
crayon
dark
daub
decorate
delineate
depict
depth
design
diagram
doodle
draft
draw
drawing
easel
egg tempera
engrave
etch
etching
facsimile
figure
focus point
foreground
frame
gallery
gesture
glaze
gouache
granite
graphic

grayed
high-key
hue
illustrate
illustration
image
impression
ink
intensity
key
landscape
layout
light
line
low-key
luminous
luster
marble
mask
masterpiece
matte
media
middle ground
miniature
mix
model
mold
mosaic
motif
mural
neutralize
nude
oil
opaque

paint
painting
palette
panorama
paper
paste-up
pastel
pattern
pedestal
pen
pencil
perspective
pictorial
picture
picturesque
pigment
plaster
portrait
portray
pose
poster
primary colors
print
profile
realism

relief
replica
representat-
 ional
rough
scale
scene
scenery
sculptor
sculpture
seascape
secondary
 colors
shade
shading
shape
silhouette
silk-screen
sketch
sketchbook
spatter
spectrum
statue
stencil
still life

stroke
studio
subdued
subject
symbol
tableau
tapestry
technique
texture
thumbnail
tint
tone
transparent
transparency
under-painting
untitled
value
view
vista
visual
visualize
wash
water media
watercolor
wax

Art Phrases

A thing of beauty is a joy forever . . . art for art's sake . . . art is long, and time is fleeting . . . draw your own conclusions . . . interior decoration . . . old master . . . one picture is worth more than a thousand words . . . painting the town red . . . plaster of paris . . . still life . . . vanishing point . . . work of art.

Entry Example

"Red Magic" describes (ketchup) because . . . though no ARTIST at cookery, I can DRAW on appetizing (ketchup) to make dinner a MASTERPIECE that turns my family into a PICTURE of contentment.

AUTOMOTIVE

4-wheel drive
18-wheeler
accelerate
accelerator
accessories
accident
air
  conditioning
alternator
anti-freeze
anti-knock
anti-lock
assembly
auto
automobile
automotive
axle
back-up
battery
bearings
blowout
body
brake
buggy
bumper
burglar alarm
bus
byway
cab
car
caravan
carburetor
caution
CB radio

cellular phone
chains
chariot
chassis
chauffeur
check-up
choke
chrome
classic
clunker
clutch
coach
collide
collision
combustion
compact
compression
continental kit
control
convertible
coupe
crank
crankcase
crash
crate
crossing
cruise control
curb
curve
cylinder
dashboard
defroster
detour
diesel

digital
dipstick
directional
distance
drain
drive
driver
driveway
emissions
engine
equipment
exhaust
fan belt
fender
fin
fine
finish
flat tire
forward
frame
freeway
fuel
gallon
garage
gas
gasoline
gauge
gears
generator
get-away
go
grease
green light
hack

hardtop
harness
headlight
heap
hearse
heater
high gear
highway
hitchhike
hood
horn
horsepower
hot rod
hub
idle
ignition
insurance
itinerary
jalopy
jaunt
jaywalk
journey
jump-start
jumper cables
key
knock
lane
lead free
leaded
lemon
license
light
limousine
low gear
lubrication
maintenance
map
mechanic

meter
mileage
model
motor
motorcycle
motorist
muffler
neutral
octane
odometer
oil
operate
overdrive
overhaul
overtake
park
parkway
parts
pass
passenger
patrol
pavement
pedal
pedestrian
phone
pick-up
piston
plug
power
pump
puncture
race
radials
radiator
red light
refill
refuel
rental car

repair
reverse
ride
road
road map
road hog
route
run
safe
safety
seat belt
sedan
semi
service
shift
shock absorber
shoulder
signal
skid
slowdown
smash-up
souped-up
spark plug
speed
speed limit
speedometer
speedway
sports car
springs
stabilizer
stall
start
starter
station
station wagon
steer
steering wheel
stop

streamline	tour	turn signal
summons	tourist	U-turn
supplies	tow	upkeep
surge	track	valve
switch	traction	van
tachometer	traffic	vehicle
tail pipe	trailer	warm-up
tail fin	transmission	water pump
tail-light	transport	wheel
take off	travel	wheelbase
tank	tread	windshield
tankful	trek	wiper
taxi	trip	wreck
thoroughfare	truck	yellow light
throttle	trunk	yield
ticket	tune-up	zone
tire	turn	
toll	turnpike	

Automotive Phrases

Assembly line . . . back-seat driver . . . behind the wheel . . . burn up the road . . . change a tire . . . change your oil . . . dangerous curves . . . emergency brake . . . fill 'er up . . . filling station . . . fix a flat . . . give 'er the gun . . . get the green light . . . gun the motor . . . hit-and-run . . . hitting on all cylinders . . . horseless carriage . . . ignition key . . . in gear . . . it's a long lane that has no turning . . . leave your motor running . . . lose your license . . . miles per gallon . . . no parking . . . parking meter . . . parking space . . . pull over to the curb . . . race the engine . . . radar detector . . . reckless driver . . . reserve power . . . retire, don't retread . . . right of way . . . road block . . . safety zone . . . self-starter . . . service station . . . sharp turn . . . shift gears . . . speed gun . . . speed trap . . . step on the gas . . . stop, look and listen . . . test run . . . thumb a ride . . .

traffic cop . . . traffic jam . . . trouble shooting . . . went into high.

Entry Examples

I like (orange juice) because . . . it's our morning STARTER whose SPARK PLUG vitamins help SPEED us through the day's activities within the SAFETY ZONE of health.

I like (toothpaste) because . . . my friends STOP, they LOOK, and I LISTEN to compliments on my whiter, brighter teeth—MOTIVE enough to use (toothpaste) regularly!

BANKING AND REAL ESTATE

account
accrue
agent
amortization
annuity
arrears
assess
asset
average
balance
balance sheet
balloon
  payment
bank
bankbook
banker
bankroll
bearer
bearish
belly-up
blue chip
bond
bondholder
bonus
bookkeeper
boom
borrow
broke
broker
budget
bullion
bullish
buy
buyer

cancelled
  check
capital
cash
cashier
cent
change
check
checkbook
checking
  account
clear
co-maker
coin
collateral
collect
combination
commercial
commission
common stock
compound
corner
cosigner
cost
count
credit
credit history
creditor
currency
debt
debtor
deduct
deed
default

deficit
deflation
deposit
depositor
dime
discount
dividend
dollar
draft
draw
due
earn
earnings
economy
embezzle
endorse
endorsement
equity
escrow
exchange
exempt
expenses
factoring
fee
federal reserve
finance
financial
fluctuate
foreign
  exchange
forge
forgery
fortune
fund

gain
gold
gross
guard
holdings
homestead
I.O.U.
income
inflation
ingot
insolvent
insurance
insure
interest
invest
investment
issue
kiting checks
lend
leverage
liability
lien
liquidate
listing
loan
lock
long-term
loss
margin
market
mature
maturity
melon
merge
mint
monetary
money
money order

monopoly
mortgage
multiple
negotiable
net
note
open house
option
overdraw
overdue
owe
par
partner
passbook
pay
payable
payment
pledge
plunge
policy
premium
price
principal
profit
profitable
promissory
promissory
note
promote
property
prospectus
proxy
purse
pyramid
quarter
quote
rally
rate

redeem
refund
repay
report
reserve
residential
resources
retirement
revenue
rich
roll
safe
save
savings
secure
security
sell
seller
share
short-term
shyster
silver
solvent
speculate
speculation
spend
statement
stock
stock market
stockholder
sum
surplus
surtax
swap
tape
tax
teller
testing

thrift	trustee	wallet
ticker	turnover	wealth
trade	underwrite	withdraw
transact	upturn	withdrawal
treasury	value	worth
treasury note	vault	yield
trust	voucher	

Banking and Real Estate Phrases

Armored car . . . blank check . . . bulls and bears . . . cancelled check . . . capital gains . . . certificate of deposit . . . clearing house . . . closing prices . . . coin of the realm . . . corner the market . . . cost of living . . . counting house . . . Easy Street . . . for sale . . . foreclose the mortgage . . . frozen assets . . . gilt edge . . . gold standard . . . high interest rate . . . income tax . . . internal revenue . . . legal tender . . . mutual funds . . . OPM (other people's money) . . . open an account . . . pay to bearer . . . pay to the order of . . . preferred stock . . . private offering . . . safety deposit box . . . sell short . . . sinking fund . . . stock exchange . . . ticker tape . . . Wall Street . . . you can bank on it.

Entry Example

I like (oil) because . . . it's made from PREFERRED STOCK corn, of PREMIUM quality, in line with (oil's) POLICY of YIELDING highest VALUE for oil INVESTMENT.

Banking Buffoonery

Lady to bank teller: "I want to open a joint account—with someone who has money."

BASEBALL

all-star	fast ball	minor league
assist	field	minors
average	fielder	mitt
backstop	first	mound
bag	flag	no-hitter
ball	fly	out
ballpark	fly ball	outfield
base	fly out	outscore
baseball	foul	pennant
bat	franchise	pitch
batter	fumble	pitcher
battery	game	plate
bench	glove	play
bleachers	grandstand	play ball
box	hit	player
bullpen	holdout	playoff
bunt	home	pop fly
call off	home plate	pop up
catch	home run	pro
catcher	homer	put out
center field	horsehide	rain check
champion	hurl	relief
clout	infield	relief pitcher
club	inning	right field
coach	lead	rookie
control	league	root
curve	left field	run
diamond	line drive	runner
double	line-up	sack
double play	liner	sacrifice
dugout	major league	safe
error	majors	score
fair	manager	scoreboard
fan	mask	scout

second	slump	throw
series	spike	tie
shortstop	stadium	trade
showers	steal	triple
shutout	strike	umpire
side	strike out	walk
signal	striking	warmup
single	swing	wild pitch
sinker	switch hitter	windup
slide	team	
slugger	third	

Baseball Phrases

At bat . . . base hit . . . base on balls . . . bases loaded . . . batting average . . . batting order . . . big league . . . bush league . . . can't get to first base . . . caught off base . . . change of pace . . . circuit clout . . . double header . . . earned run . . . farm team . . . first division . . . foul ball . . . foul line . . . four-bagger . . . go to the showers . . . grandstand play . . . Hall of Fame . . . hit the dirt . . . hits home . . . hitting power . . . home team . . . it's a hit . . . knock out of the box . . . last of the ninth . . . major league . . . make the play . . . national pastime . . . no hits, no runs, no errors . . . on the road . . . one-bagger . . . out of his league . . . over the fence . . . pinch hitter . . . play ball! . . . second division . . . seventh inning stretch . . . slow ball . . . Spring training . . . squeeze play . . . steal a base . . . steal home . . . stolen base . . . three-bagger . . . two strikes on him . . . winning run . . . winning streak . . . World Series.

Entry Example

(Car) is America's most popular compact car because . . . it SCORES a HIT with thrift-minded FANS from all WALKS of life who are BATTY about its MAJOR performance at MINOR price.

BASKETBALL

air ball
assist
assistant coach
back board
back court
bank shot
base line
basketball
bench
block
center
centerline
champion
championship
charging
clock
coach
court
defense
defensive team
double dribble
down court
dribble
fast break
floor
forward

foul
foul out
foul trouble
free throw
free throw line
game
glass
goal tending
guard
hook shot
hoop
illegal defense
jump
jump shot
key
layup
league
line
loss
net
offense
offensive foul
offensive team
out of bounds
over and back
overtime

pass in
pass
playoffs
practice
press
pushing
reaching
referee
regular season
rim
score
set shot
shoot
shot
sideline
slam dunk
swish
team
teammates
technical
technical shot
travel
up and over
up court
victory

Basketball Phrases

Floor it . . . foul-mouthed . . . I was floored . . . jump ball . . . make a pass . . . practice makes perfect . . . toe the line . . . working overtime.

Illustration

When you SHOOT off your mouth, you COURT disaster, put people in a FOUL mood, and get everybody on the DEFENSIVE.

BIRDS

aerie	dove	nest
albatross	down	nestling
aviary	duck	nightingale
bantam	duckling	ostrich
beak	eagle	owl
biddy	egg	parakeet
bill	falcon	parrot
bird	feather	partridge
birdbath	feathery	peacock
birdcall	flight	peahen
blue jay	flock	peep
bluebird	fly	pelican
breed	fowl	penguin
brood	game	perch
buzzard	glide	pigeon
cackle	gobbler	plumage
cage	goose	plume
canary	gosling	poultry
cardinal	grouse	preen
caw	gull	pullet
cheep	hatch	quack
chicken	hawk	quail
claw	hen	quill
cock	heron	raven
cockatiel	hoot	robin
cockatoo	hummingbird	roost
coo	incubate	rooster
covey	jay	sing
crane	kiwi	soar
crest	lark	songster
crow	loon	sparrow
cuckoo	lovebird	squab
cygnet	migrate	stork
dodo	molt	swallow

swan	toucan	wing
swift	turkey	wishbone
talon	vulture	woodpecker
tern	warble	wren

Bird Phrases

A bird in the hand is worth two in the bush . . .
bill and coo . . . bird of prey . . . bird's eye view . . .
birds of a feather flock together . . . chicken feed . . .
crazy as a loon . . . dead as a dodo . . . early bird
catches the worm . . . eat crow . . . feather your nest .
. . fine feathered friend . . . get the bird . . . homing
pigeon . . . proud as a peacock . . . push them out of
the nest . . . sitting duck . . . soft as down . . . stool
pigeon . . . swan song . . . talk turkey . . . wise as an
owl.

Entry Example

I take (antacid) because . . . when headache gets
me DOWN, just one SWALLOW puts misery to
FLIGHT, makes pain take WING, and leaves me
happy as a LARK.

BOATING

aboard
admiral
adrift
afloat
aft
aloft
amidship
anchor
aweigh
bail
ballast
barometer
bay
beach
beacon
beam
bearings
berth
bilge
boat
boatman
bow
bridge
brine
bulkhead
bulwark
bunk
buoy
cabin
calm
canoe
canvas
capsize
captain

cargo
castaway
channel
chart
clipper
coast
cockpit
command
commodore
compass
course
craft
crew
cruise
cruiser
current
deck
deckhand
derelict
dinghy
disembark
dock
draft
drift
drown
dry dock
embark
fathom
flagship
fleet
float
flood
flotilla
foam

forecastle
forward
freighter
galley
gangplank
gangway
gear
gob
ground
gulf
hail
harbor
hatch
helm
helmsman
hold
horizon
houseboat
hull
jettison
keel
ketch
knot
lake
landlubber
launch
league
lee
leeward
life belt
life jacket
life preserver
life raft
lifeboat

lighthouse
liner
list
locker
log
lookout
marine
mariner
maritime
maroon
mast
master
mate
mess
moor
mooring
motorboat
mutiny
nautical
naval
navigate
navy
oar
ocean
outboard
overboard
paddle
paddle boat
paddle wheel
pier
pilot
piracy
pirate
pond
port
porthole
propeller
purser

raft
reef
rigging
river
row
rowboat
rudder
runabout
sail
sailor
salvage
schooner
scow
scuttle
scuttlebutt
sea
seafaring
seagoing
seaman
seamanship
seasick
seaway
seaworthy
sextant
shanghai
ship
shipshape
shipwreck
shoal
shore
showboat
sink
skiff
skipper
sloop
SOS
sounding
spar

splice
squadron
starboard
stateroom
steamboat
steamer
steer
steersman
stern
storm
stowaway
strand
stream
submarine
surf
swamp
swell
swim
tack
tar
tide
tiller
topside
tub
vessel
voyage
wake
water
waterline
waterway
wave
weather
wharf
wheel
windward
yacht
yawl

Boating Phrases

Able seaman . . . all at sea . . . all hands on deck . . . anchors aweigh . . . any port in a storm . . . aye, aye, sir! . . . batten down the hatches . . . bon voyage! . . . both in the same boat . . . cast off . . . chart a course . . . clear the deck . . . coast is clear . . . Davy Jones' locker . . . dead reckoning . . . distress signal . . . don't give up the ship . . . ebb tide . . . flotsam and jetsam . . . flying colors . . . from stem to stern . . . full speed ahead . . . give it a wide berth . . . high and dry . . . high seas . . . hit the deck . . . hoist your sails . . . life preserver . . . man overboard . . . naval maneuvers . . . old salt . . . paddle your own canoe . . . put in your oar . . . safe harbor . . . set a course . . . ship ahoy! . . . sink or swim . . . smooth sailing . . . slow boat to China . . . take the wind out of his sails . . . trim your sails . . . under full sail . . . under way . . . walk the plank.

Entry Example

"I choose (cigarette) because . . . I was a cigarette SKIPPER till (cigarette) PILOTED me to the right PORT with a SMOOTH-SAILING smoke that always gives me GOBS of pleasure."

BOWLING

aim	grip	release
alley	groove	return
angle	gutter	roll
approach	headpin	runway
backswing	hit	score
balk	hook	setup
ball	kegler	shoes
bowl	kingpin	shot
bowler	lane	slide
bowling	league	span
champion	leave	spare
control	lift	spin
course	line	split
curve	mark	sport
delivery	match	stance
downswing	momentum	step
finger	pastime	stoop
follow-through	pin	strike
footwork	pit	swing
form	play	team
frame	pocket	tenpins
game	pushaway	thumb

Bowling Phrases

Anchor man . . . body English . . . bowl over . . . down the alley . . . foul line . . . he stoops to conquer (conk'er) . . . in the groove . . . into the gutter . . . knock down . . . lead off . . . lead pin . . . make a strike . . . on the nose . . . on the spot . . . perfect 300 . . . right up your alley . . . roll off . . . set 'em up . . . spare time . . . strike it rich . . . thumb fun!

Entry Example

I enjoy (magazine) because . . . its humor BOWLS me over, for nothing is SPARED in its attempts to STRIKE me funny and make me SPLIT my sides with laughter!

BOXING

amateur
antagonist
arena
back-pedal
bantam
bash
batter
battle
beat
beat-up
bell
belt
black eye
block
blow
body blow
bop
bout
box
boxer
boxing
brawl
breadbasket
break
bruiser
button
canvas
card
cauliflower ear
challenge
challenger
champ
champion
championship

chop
clinch
clip
clout
come to
comeback
conk
connect
conquer
contender
contest
corner
count
counter
counter punch
crown
cuff
daze
decision
defeat
defense
defensive
disqualify
dive
dodge
draw
drop
dukes
exhibition
fair
fake
featherweight
feint
fight

fighter
fist
fistic
fisticuffs
flatten
floor
flyweight
fold up
footwork
foul
gate
Gate receipts
gladiator
glove
guard
ham
handle
handler
haymaker
heavyweight
hit
hook
jab
jolt
judge
knockdown
knockout
knuckles
KO
lead
left
lightweight
long count
lose

loser
low blow
manage
manager
match
matchmaker
mauler
middleweight
miss
mix
mouthpiece
nail
opponent
outpoint
parry
paste
plaster
poke
preliminary
prizefight
prizefighter
professional
promoter
pug
pugilist
pummel
punch
punch-drunk

puncher
punching bag
punchy
punishment
pushover
quit
quitter
rally
reach
referee
right
ring
ringside
ringside seat
ropes
round
roundhouse
rusty
scrap
second
setup
shiner
short count
slam-bang
slap-happy
slug
slugger
smack

sock
spar
sparring
  partner
sport
stagger
stooge
stop
strike
stumblebum
swing
technical
  knock-out
thump
tilt
title
title fight
TKO
train
trainer
trunks
tussle
uppercut
verdict
wallop
weight
win
winner

Boxing Phrases

After the brawl is over . . . art of self-defense . . .
bare knuckles . . . battle of the century . . . battle
royal . . . beat to the punch . . . below the belt . . .
between rounds . . . chopping block . . . clenched fist .
. . come out fighting . . . count out . . . defend for the
crown . . . double-cross . . . double up . . . down but

not out . . . down for the count . . . drawing card . . .
fair blow . . . fighting fool . . . fighting mad . . . fix a
fight . . . fixed fight . . . foul blow . . . free for all . . .
get on the bicycle . . . get the nod . . . glass jaw . . .
glutton for punishment . . . go the distance . . . Golden Glover . . . grudge fight . . . hang up the gloves . . .
hit the deck (or mat) . . . horizontal fighter . . . in the
bag . . . in the pink of condition . . . kiss the canvas . .
. knock for a loop . . . lead with the chin . . . leading
contender . . . leather-pusher . . . main event . . .
manly art . . . Marquis of Queensberry Rules . . .
neutral corner . . . on the button . . . on the level . . .
on the ropes . . . one-two punch . . . out cold . . . out
like a light . . . out of his feet . . . Pack a wallop . . .
pier six brawl . . . pull a punch . . . put on the gloves .
. . put up your dukes . . . rabbit punch . . . raise the
winner's hand . . . roll with a punch . . . roundhouse
swing . . . see stars . . . saved by the bell . . . shadow
box . . . slugging match . . . strike back . . . Sunday
punch . . . take a dive . . . take it on the chin . . . take
the count . . . telegraph a punch . . . ten and out . . .
throw in the towel (or sponge) . . . time out . . . training quarters . . . two-fisted . . . unanimous decision . .
. weigh in . . . white hope . . . wild swing . . . win by a
decision . . . win, lose or draw . . . win on points . . .
world champion.

Entry Example

"I like (soap) because . . . there's enough PUNCH
in these CHAMPION suds to KNOCK OUT dirt
from even HEAVYWEIGHT wash, yet they're kind
to FLYWEIGHT fabrics."

BUILDING

abode
adhesive
air condition
alcove
alter
alteration
aluminum
annex
anteroom
apartment
appliances
arch
architect
area
asphalt
attic
awl
awning
axe
backyard
balcony
base
basement
bathroom
beam
bedrock
bedroom
bind
blind
block
blueprint
board
boiler
bolt

bond
bottom
brace
brad
brass
break ground
brick
bricklayer
bridge
buckle
build
builder
building
bulldozer
bungalow
buttress
cabin
cabinet
calk
canopy
carpenter
carpet
castle
cathedral
ceiling
cellar
cement
chamber
chimney
city
clapboard
clay
closet
column

completion
concrete
construct
construction
copper
cornerstone
cornice
corridor
cottage
court
crane
decor
decorate
decorator
demolish
derrick
design
develop
development
dig
digs
dimension
dinette
dining room
dome
domicile
door
doorway
dovetail
draft
drafting
drainage
duplex
dwelling

eaves
edifice
elevator
engineer
entrance
erect
erection
estate
excavate
excavation
exterior
fabricate
facade
facia
facing
fasten
faucet
fence
fiber
file
fill
finish
fixture
floor
floor plan
foundation
foyer
frame
frontage
furnace
furnish
furnishings
garage
girder
glass
grade
granite
great room

ground
gutter
gypsum
hall
hallway
hammer
hardware
header
hew
high
home
horizontal
house
household
incinerator
indoor
install
installation
insulation
interior
jamb
joint
key
keystone
kitchen
ladder
land
landlord
landscape
latch
lath
lawn
layout
lease
level
lift
living room
lobby

lock
loft
lot
lumber
mansion
mantel
marble
mason
masonry
metal
model home
molding
mortar
mortgage
move
nail
niche
nut
occupy
outdoor
paint
palace
palatial
pane
panel
pantry
parapet
partition
passage
patio
pavement
pillar
pipe
pitch
plan
plank
plaster
plastic

plumb
plumber
plumbing
porch
post
project
property
pulley
putty
pyramid
quarry
rafter
rail
raise
raze
realtor
rent
rental
repair
residence
residential
rivet
roof
room
saw
scaffold
screen
screw
setback
sewer
shade
shanty
shelf

shelter
shingle
shovel
shutter
siding
sill
sink
site
skyscraper
slate
solid
space
span
specification
spike
split level
square
square footage
stairs
steel
steps
stone
story
structure
strut
stucco
studio
suburbs
support
surface
survey
tall
tar

tear down
tenant
tenement
terrace
threshold
tile
timber
tool
top
tower
town
tract
tradesperson
trim
trowel
vacancy
vacant
varnish
veranda
vertical
vestibule
village
wall
wallpaper
weld
window
wood
woodwork
wrench
yard
zone

Building Phrases

A house is a home . . . all modern conveniences . . . big build up . . . brace and bit . . . bricks without straw . . . concrete mixer . . . do it yourself . . . earth moving equipment . . . empty log . . . fire escape . . . from cellar to attic . . . from top to bottom . . . front porch . . . groundbreaking ceremony . . . high, wide and handsome . . . hit the ceiling . . . home improvement . . . home owner . . . home, sweet home . . . house that Jack built . . . interior decorator . . . lay the foundation . . . living quarters . . . moving van . . . no trespassing . . . nuts and bolts . . . pile driver . . . planning stage . . . raw materials . . . real estate . . . sidewalk superintendent . . . solid foundation . . . southern exposure . . . steam roller . . . steam shovel . . . there's no place like home!

Entry Example

"I like the new (car) because . . . CONSTRUCTED with skill and BUILT to last, this latest DEVELOPMENT in automobile DESIGN is ENGINEERED to deliver CEILING value at BEDROCK price."

BUSINESS AND SALES

account
acquisition
administration
advertise
advertisement
agency
aisle
annual report
apprentice
associates
autocratic
bag
bargain
benefits
bill
bounce back
boutique
box
brand
brochure
brown nose
brown nosing
budget
business
buy
buyer
C.O.D.
capital
carton
cash
cash flow
cash register
cashier
CEO

change
charge account
cheap
checkout
classify
clearance
clerk
client
close out
commerce
commercial
commission
commitment
company
competition
competitor
consumer
contract
cost
counter
credit
credit card
customer
customer
  service
cut-rate
damage
deal
dealer
delegate
delivery
department
department
  store

direct mail
directors
discount
display
economy
embellish
empire
employ
employees
enterprise
entrepreneur
exchange
expansion
expense
expensive
financial
  statement
fixture
flyer
FOB
forecast
franchise
good buy
goods
gross
guarantee
half off
help
hire
income
incubator
intern
inventory
job

job description
label
leader
line
liquidation
loss
mail-order
mall
manager
managerial
mannequin
manufacturing
markdown
market
marketing
marketplace
markup
mart
memo
mercantile
merchandise
merchant
merger
nepotism
net
office politics
operation
order
organization
organizational
  chart
outlet
overcharge
overhead
own
owner
P&L
package

pamphlet
parcel
partners
patron
patronize
pay
paycheck
payment
payroll
pension
plan
policy manual
positioning
premium
price
price point
price tag
prioritizing
priority
proceeds
produce
product
production
profit
profitable
promotion
proposal
proprietor
public pur-
chase
purchase order
quality control
receipt
recruiting
reduce
refund
relations
remnant space

resale
retail
ring up
risk
salary
sale
sales
sales slip
salesperson
save
savings
savvy
scatter
security
sell
serve
service
shelf
ship
shop
shopping
show
showroom
shrewd
sign
skill
space
special
spend
staff
stock
store
storekeeper
substitute
supervisor
supplier
supply
survival

takeover	value	wholesale
team spirit	variety	window
telemarketing	vender	work force
thrift	venture capital	working capital
trade	wait on	wrap
transaction	warehouse	
tycoon	wares	

Business and Sales Phrases

All sold out . . . bargain basement . . . behind the counter . . . Better Business Bureau . . . blowing smoke . . . board of directors . . . break even point . . . buy now, pay later . . . capital investment . . . cash accounting . . . cash and carry . . . cash on delivery . . . chain of command . . . charge it . . . close the sale . . . comparison shopping . . . debt service . . . do it yourself . . . down payment . . . 80/20 rule . . . fill the bill . . . fire sale . . . first come, first served . . . floor walker . . . Fortune 500 . . . human resources development . . . general store . . . gift-wrapped . . . going out-of-business sale . . . good will . . . high-pressure salesmanship . . . if you don't see what you want, ask for it . . . incentive plan . . . industry standards . . . installment plan . . . lean and mean . . . let the buyer beware . . . line of credit . . . management team . . . massaging the numbers . . . mission statement . . . money cheerfully refunded . . . money's worth . . . nothing happens until somebody sells something . . . on the shelf . . . over the counter . . . profit and loss . . . quick and dirty . . . raise the price . . . retirement plan . . . revenue stream . . . ring up a sale . . . sales check . . . sales talk . . . self-service . . . supply and demand . . . sweetheart deal . . . take inventory . . . the customer is always right . . . The Peter Principle . . . the price is right . . . today's big special . . . unit production cost . .

. under the counter . . . untouched by human hands . .
. vertical integration . . . worth the price.

Store Story

Shopping in a department store, a very stout woman
asked a bow-legged clerk where talcum powder was sold.
"Just walk this way, madam," he guided her. She re-
sponded: "If I could walk that way, I wouldn't need any
talcum powder!

Business Banter

Successful people have a strong will. Lazy people
have a strong won't.

CARD GAMES

ace
ante
auction
bank
banker
bet
bettor
bid
bidder
black
blackjack
bluff
bonus
bridge
build
call
canasta
card
chance
cheat
chip
club
concede
contract
count
cribbage
cut
deal
dealer
deck
deuce
diamond
discard
draw

dummy
euchre
face
face card
faro
finesse
flush
forfeit
full
full house
gamble
game
gin
grand
hand
heart
hearts
honors
IOU
jack
jackpot
joker
kibitzer
king
kitty
knock
layout
lead
limit
lose
luck
mark
marriage
matchstick

meld
misdeal
odds
old maid
open
opener
opponent
pack
pair
partner
pass
pat
penalty
penny
pinochle
pitch
play
player
point
poker
pot
queen
raise
red
renege
revoke
riffle
risk
round
royal
royal flush
rubber
rummy
score

see	spot	talon
sequence	spread	thump
seven up	stack	trey
shark	stakes	trick
show	stay	turn
showdown	stock	twenty-one
shuffle	straight	vulnerable
side	straight flush	wager
slam	stud	whist
solitaire	suit	win
spade	sweep	

Card Game Phrases

Ace high . . . ace in the hole . . . at stake . . . beginner's luck . . . blue chip . . . card sharp . . . chips are down . . . cut the cards . . . deuces wild . . . easy mark . . . face down . . . face up . . . follow suit . . . four of a kind . . . freeze out . . . gin rummy . . . go for broke . . . good hand . . . grand slam . . . hearts are trumps . . . high card . . . high stakes . . . inside straight . . . lead with the ace, king, queen, etc . . . little slam . . . lucky at cards, unlucky in love . . . marked deck . . . playing card . . . poker face . . . sky's the limit . . . slap jack . . . stacked deck . . . stand pat . . . strip poker . . . table stakes . . . three of a kind . . . top card . . . two pairs . . . under the table . . . up my sleeve . . . winning hand.

Entry Example

"I always trade at (store) because . . . their ACE-high products are fit for KING or QUEEN, yet my 'JACK' always gets a square DEAL."

Slogan Sample

"A CLUB with a HEART to SPADE up prize DIA-
MONDS."

CHESS
(including Checkers and related terms)

advance
advantage
attack
beat
beginner
bishop
block
blunder
board
capture
castle
caution
challenge
champion
check
checkers
checkmate
chess
chessboard
chessman
color
concentrate
corner
counter
crown
defeat
defend
defense
development
diagonal
draw
enemy
exchange

expert
file
force
fork
forward
gambit
game
give up
guard
horse
hostile
interpose
jump
king
knight
lose
loser
man
maneuver
master
mate
menace
mobility
movable
move
objective
offense
opponent
opposition
parry
partner
pastime
patience

pawn
penalize
penalty
piece
pin
pitfall
play
player
position
problem
promote
promotion
protect
queen
rank
remove
resign
rook
row
sacrifice
score
shield
skill
square
stalemate
stock
strategy
surrender
tactics
take
technique
threattie
tournament

trap   win   yield
versus   winner
victor   withdraw

Chess Phrases

Against odds . . . all even . . . best move . . . black piece . . . capture a piece . . . . checker board . . . concede defeat . . . clean sweep . . . counter attack . . . double attack . . . double check . . . end game . . . equal strength . . . even exchange . . . fair exchange is no loss . . . favorable position . . . get a king . . . guard the king . . . in check . . . it's your move . . . king's row . . . long live the king . . . move into action . . . on the defense . . . opening move . . . opening position . . . perpetual check . . . queen a pawn . . . rank and file . . . relative value . . . royal game . . . superior force . . . take the offensive . . . white piece . . . win, lose or draw . . . winning combination.

Entry Example

I shop at (store) because . . . by CHECKING values, I've found my smartest MOVE was to (store), always on the SQUARE and above BOARD, pleasing me and my MATE.

CHILDREN

adolescence
adolescent
baby
baby sitter
bald
bib
bicycle
bottle
brat
bubble gum
bunk beds
burp
change
child
child care
childhood
childish
christen
color books
cradle
crawl
crayons
crib
crybaby
cuddle
darling
diaper
diaper rash
discipline

doll
finger paints
formula
gun
highchair
immaturity
infant
innocence
juvenile
kid
kindergarten
latchkey
layette
little
lullaby
minor
newborn
nursery school
pacifier
pamper
playground
potty train
preschool
puberty
rascal
rocking horse
rocking chair
roller skate
sandbox

school
schoolyard
small
snuggle
spank
spoil
stories
strained food
stroller
swing set
teddy bear
teen
teenager
teething
thumb sucking
tinker toys
tiny
toddler
tot
toy
train
training pants
tricycle
tyke
walker
wet
youngster

Children Phrases

Best bib and tucker . . . curtain climber . . . don't kid around . . . from cradle to grave . . . good things come in small packages . . . house ape . . . Jack and Jill went up the hill . . . let your child out . . . spare the rod, spoil the child . . . what a doll! . . . you're all wet.

Corporate Profile

(Company) is a perfect example of how new businesses are BORN to fill a need. As with any INFANT there were GROWING PAINS. But soon the YOUNG-STER was ambling along on STEADY LEGS.

Child Chatter

He was so ugly when he was born the doctor slapped his mother.

When children are small, *we* think they're brilliant. When they become teenagers, *they* think we're retarded.

CLOTHING

accessories
alter
alteration
apparel
apron
armhole
attire
B.V.D.s
baste
becoming
belt
beret
bib
blazer
blouse
bodice
bolt
bonnet
boot
bow
bow tie
bowler
boxer
breeches
brim
broadcloth
buckle
buckskin
button
buttonhole
calico
camisole
camouflage
cap

cape
checks
chic
chiffon
clad
closet
cloth
clothe
clothes
coat
collar
color
corset
costume
cotton
cravat
crease
crochet
crown
cuff
cut
cutaway
dandy
denim
derby
design
dickey
disrobe
doff
doll up
don
double
   breasted
drape

drawers
dress
dressmaker
duck
dude
duds
dummy
dye
embroider
ensemble
evening dress
eyelet
fabric
fancy
fashion
fasten
fastener
fedora
felt
fiber
figure
finish
fit
fitting
flair
flannel
flare
fleece
footwear
fop
formal
foundation
fray
frill

frock
fur
gabardine
gaiter
galluses
galoshes
garment
garter
gauntlet
gingham
girdle
glamour
glove
gown
groom
hanger
hat
hem
hemline
hood
hose
hosiery
iron
jacket
jeans
jersey
kid
kidskin
kilts
knickers
knit
lace
lapel
laundry
leather
linen
lingerie
lining

links
look
mannequin
match
material
measure
mend
mesh
mini
mitten
moccasin
mode
model
modish
mohair
muff
muffler
muslin
nap
neckline
necktie
needle
nightgown
notions
nylon
outfit
overalls
overcoat
pad
padding
pajamas
pants
panty
parka
patch
pattern
pin
piping

plaid
pleat
plush
ply
pocket
polyester
preppie
press
prewashed
prints
pump
rags
raiment
raincoat
ramie
rayon
ribbon
rip
ritzy
robe
sandal
sash
satin
scarf
scissors
seam
serge
sew
shabby
shape
shawl
shears
sheer
shell
shirt
shod
shoe
shorts

shrink
silk
single breasted
size
skirt
slacks
sleeve
slicker
slip
slipper
snap
sneakers
snug
socks
sole
spats
spinstitch
stocking
strap
strapless
strip
stripe
style
stylish
suede
suit
suspenders
swanky

swatch
sweater
swimsuit
tailor
tailor-made
tails
tap pants
tape measure
tear
teddy
textile
texture
thread
tie
tights
togs
topcoat
tricot
trim
trimming
trousers
trousseau
trunks
tuck
tux
tuxedo
tweed
twill

ulster
underwear
undress
uniform
V-neck
veil
velvet
vest
visor
waist
waistline
wardrobe
wash and wear
wear
wearable
weave
western
wool
woolen
worn
worsted
woven
wrinkle
yarn
yoke
zipper

Clothing Phrases

A stitch in time saves nine . . . all dressed up and no place to go . . . Beau Brummel . . . best bib and tucker . . . birthday suit . . . button up your overcoat . . . buttons and bows . . . clothes horse . . . clothes make the man . . . doff your hat . . . Dr. Denton's dotted swiss . . . dressed to kill . . . dry goods . . . evening clothes . .

. false front . . . fill his shoes . . . fine feathers made fine birds . . . flair for fashion . . . foundation garment . . . from rags to riches . . . full dress . . . girth control . . . girth of a nation . . . give a darn . . . glad rags . . . go formal . . . golden fleece . . . gone to waist . . . hand-me-downs . . . high hat . . . high, wide and handsome . . . hot under the collar . . . keep it under your hat . . . kid gloves . . . Little Red Riding Hood . . . made to order . . . mend your ways . . . never say dye . . . nip and tuck . . . not a thing to wear . . . old clothes man . . . padded shoulders . . . pins and needles . . . pocket your pride . . . polka dots . . . press his suit . . . put on your thinking cap . . . putting on the Ritz . . . ready made . . . ready to wear . . . Sam, you made the pants too long . . . sew it seams . . . snug fit . . . soup and fish . . . strip tease . . . stuffed shirt . . . take your hat off to him . . . top hat, white tie and tails . . . try this on for size . . . union suit . . . waist measure . . . wear out . . . wear the pants in your family . . . well-heeled . . . what the well-dressed executive will wear . . . white glove test . . . wolf in sheep's clothing . . . wool gathering . . . your slip is showing.

Entry Example

My favorite (frozen food) is mixed vegetables because . . . springtime COLORS, appetizing SHAPES, forkable SIZES, and tempting TEXTURES are SUITABLY blended to FASHION fresh five-piece ENSEMBLES.

COLORS

amber	ebony	navy
apricot	emerald	neutral
auburn	fade	olive
azure	fair	orange
black	fawn	pale
bleach	flame	pastel
blond	flaxen	peach
blue	flesh	pearl
blues	florid	piebald
brassy	flush	pigment
bright	gaudy	pink
brilliant	gild	platinum
bronze	gilt	plum
brown	glow	primary
brunette	gold	primary color
buff	golden	prism
canary	gray	prismatic
carmine	green	purple
chartreuse	harmonize	rainbow
claret	hazel	raven
clash	hue	red
clear	indigo	redden
colorful	iridescent	rose
colorless	ivory	roseate
copper	jet	rosy
coral	khaki	rouge
cream	lavender	royal blue
crimson	lemon	ruby
dark	light	ruddy
deep	lilac	russet
drab	loden	sable
dull	maroon	sandy
dusky	mauve	sapphire
dye	natural	scarlet

secondary
secondary
  color
shade
shocking
silver
silvery
sky-blue

spectrum
stain
swarthy
tan
tawny
tinge
tint
tone

verdant
vermilion
violet
vivid
white
whitewash
yellow

Color Phrases

Black and blue . . . black magic . . . blackout . . . blue laws . . . blue moon . . . coal black . . . do it up brown . . . feel blue . . . get the greet light . . . gild the lily . . . golden rule . . . golden West . . . green around the gills . . . green-eyed monster . . . in the pink . . . in the red . . . jet black . . . long green . . . off-white . . . olive drab . . . out of the red . . . red as a beet . . . red herring . . . red hot . . . red tape . . . red, white and blue . . . rose-colored glasses . . . see red . . . snow-white . . . treat him white . . . true-blue . . . wearing of the green . . . white as snow . . . white feather . . . yellow journalism . . . yellow streak.

Entry Example

My family prefers (cereal) because . . . they're true-BLUE value from the GOLDEN WEST, turn DARK BROWN mornings into ROSY dawns, keep our health in the PINK and our budget out of the RED.

COMPUTERS

access
applications
backup
buffer
bulletin board
byte
cancel
chip
clone
codes
computer
control
controller
crash
cursor
daisy wheel
data entry
database
default
delete
desk top
directory
disc drive
diskette
display
document
dot matrix
download
error
escape
exit
file
floppy

font
format
function
graphics
hacker
hard copy
hard disc
hardware
help
index
input
integrated
interface
keyboard
language
laptop
laser
letter quality
load
macro
main frame
megabyte
memory
memory chip
menu
merge
message
micro
mini
modem
monitor
mother board
mouse

network
novice
operating
 system
output
PC
peripheral
printer
printout
program
RAM
random
re-boot
reset
ROM
save
screen
search
setup
software
spell check
spreadsheet
system
systems
 analysis
terminal
turnkey
upgrade
user
utility
word
 processing
work station

Computer Phrases

All systems go . . . I get the message . . . make a graceful exit . . . quiet as a mouse . . . silver screen . . . save your breath . . . take a load off my mind . . . the language of love . . . user friendly.

Fictional Characterization

Her MEMORY was like a COMPUTER. She methodically FILED everything away, then CALLED IT UP with LASER speed.

COOKING

add
bake
baker
barbecue
baste
batter
beat
bit
blend
boil
brew
broil
brown
carve
charcoal
chef
chop
chunk
coals
combine
concoction
condiment
convection
cook
cooking
crumble
crush
cube
cup
cut
dash
dice
dilute
divide

dollop
dough
drain
enhance
flavor
freeze
fry
garnish
gourmet
grate
grease
greasy
grill
grind
ingredients
juice
knead
liquid
lump
marinade
mash
measure
melt
microwave
mince
mix
mixture
morsel
nuke
oil
pare
peel
pepper
piece

pinch
portion
prepare
process
pulp
recipe
reduce
relish
rind
rise
roast
roll
rub
salt
saute
scald
scrape
scrub
sear
season
serve
shave
sieve
sift
simmer
sizzle
skin
slab
slice
soften
spice
squeeze
steam
steep

stew	taste	wedge
stir	teaspoon	whip
stomach	toast	whisk
strain	trim	zest
tablespoon	warm	

Cooking Phrases

An army marches on its stomach . . . brown 'n serve . . . bump and grind . . . cut it out . . . mix 'n match . . . my cup runneth over . . . rub him the wrong way . . . rub me the wrong way . . . salt of the earth . . . Senate minority whip . . . slice of life . . . take your lumps . . . too many cooks spoil the broth.

Dialogue

"You really don't MINCE words, do you?" he exclaimed. "I don't RELISH being treated like I don't have a DOLLOP of sense! You could at least SOFTEN you voice so I wouldn't feel like ROASTING you over hot COALS."

COWBOYS

ambush	chuck wagon	heifer
badge	cinch	herd
badlands	claim	highwayman
badman	colt	hogtie
bandanna	corral	holster
bandit	covered wagon	hombre
bar	cow	homestead
bison	cowboy	horse
blockhouse	cowgirl	horseman
bonanza	cowpoke	Indian
boots	cowpuncher	lariat
bounty	critter	lasso
brand	deputy	lawman
bridle	desperado	livestock
bronco	dogie	loco
buck	draw	longhorn
buckaroo	drive	lope
buckboard	drover	lynch
buckskin	dude	marksman
buffalo	dude ranch	marshal
bull	fence	maverick
bulldogger	frontier	mount
bullet	frontiersman	mustang
bunkhouse	gallop	nester
burro	gamble	noose
calf	graze	outfit
camp	grubstake	outlaw
campfire	gulch	pack
cattle	gun	pasture
cattleman	gunfight	pinto
cayuse	gunfighter	pioneer
chaps	gunfire	pistol
chow	halter	plains
chuck	hands	poke

pommel
pony
posse
prairie
pronto
prospector
quirt
ranch
range
ranger
rawhide
reach
reins
ride
rifle
roan
rodeo
rope

roundup
rustle
rustler
saddle
saddlebag
sagebrush
saloon
settler
sheriff
shoot
shot
shotgun
six-gun
six-shooter
sombrero
sourdough
spurs
stagecoach

stampede
steer
stirrup
stock
stockman
stray
tenderfoot
tie
trail
trigger
tumbleweed
vamoose
varmint
vigilant
wagon train
West
western
wrangler

Cowboy Phrases

Boots and saddle . . . bite the dust . . . bounty hunter . . . branding iron . . . break a horse . . . bronco buster . . . bury me not on the lone prairie . . . Chisholm Trail . . . deep in the heart of Texas . . . don't fence me in . . . drugstore cowboy . . . fastest gun in the West . . . get the drop on . . . Girl of the Golden West . . . get along, little dogie . . . goodbye, Old Paint . . . go west, young man . . . grab the bull by the horns . . . great train robbery . . . gun down . . . have gun, will travel . . . hitching post . . . home on the range . . . jump a chain . . . kit and caboodle . . . last frontier . . . last roundup . . . lead poisoning . . . mess wagon . . . no man's land . . . out to lynch . . . out where the West begins . . . plumb loco . . . pony express . . . quick on the draw . . . quick on the trigger . . . ride 'em, cowboy . . . ride herd . . . rope and tie . . . see what the boys in the back room

will have . . . smile when you call me that . . . tall grass
country . . . ten gallon hat . . . thar's gold in them thar
hills . . . the Great Divide . . . the Oregon Trail . . .
throw the bull . . . thundering herd . . . trail boss . . .
two-gun man . . . under Western skies . . . wagon wheels
. . . war paint . . . wide open spaces . . . wild and woolly
. . . wild West.

Entry Example

I feed my dog (dog food) . . . it's the BRAND with
ROPE 'EM IN flavor, full RANGE of vitamins, and a
ROUNDUP of the meatiest dog-DRAWING FIXIN'S
—BAR none!

CRIME

abduct
abscond
abuse
accessory
accomplice
accuse
addict
alibi
ambush
ammunition
appeal
armed
arrest
arsenal
arson
attack
attorney
autopsy
bad
badge
badman
bail
bandit
bar
beat
billy
blackjack
blackmail
bloodhound
bobby
body
boodle
bootlegger
booty

bounty
bribe
brig
bullet
bump off
burglar
burglar alarm
cage
capital
   punishment
captive
capture
cartridge
case
catch
cell
cheat
club
clue
collar
commit
commutation
commute
con man
confess
convict
conviction
cooler
coop
cop
copper
coroner
corpse
counterfeit

court
courtroom
crime
criminal
crook
crooked
culprit
defend
defraud
delinquent
deputy
detective
dick
disarm
disguise
district
   attorney
dossier
dragnet
drugs
electric chair
embezzle
enforce
enforcement
escape
evidence
evil
execution
extortion
false arrest
fatal
FBI
felon
felony

fence
fine
fingerprint
firebug
fleece
forge
forgery
fraud
frisk
fugitive
G-man
gallows
gamble
gang
gangster
getaway
grand jury
grand larceny
grapevine
guilt
guilty
gun
gyp
handcuff
hands up
hang
hangout
harass
headquarters
highwayman
hijack
holdup
homicide
hoodlum
identify
illegal
implicate
imprisonment

incest
incriminate
inmate
innocent
inspector
jail
jailbird
jimmy
judge
jug
juvenile
   delinquent
justice
kidnap
kill
lam
larceny
launder
law
lawless
lawyer
legal
lie detector
life sentence
lifer
lock
loot
lynch
maim
manhunt
marshal
mask
mayhem
misdemeanor
mob
molest
motive
mug

mugger
murder
mutiny
narcotics
neighborhood
   watch
nightstick
number
offend
offender
offense
officer
outlaw
paddy wagon
padlock
pardon
parole
patrol
patrolman
pen
penal
penalty
penitentiary
pickpocket
piece
pinch
pirate
pistol
poison
police
policeman
posse
precinct
prison
probation
prohibit
prohibition
prosecute

prosecutor
punish
pusher
racket
ransom
rape
reprieve
revolver
rifle
rob
robber
rogue
safe
safecracker
scoundrel
search
search warrant
self-defense
sentence
shackle
shadow
shield
shoot
Sing Sing
siren
slay
sleuth

slug
smuggle
solution
solve
spy
squeal
stay
steal
stickup
stool pigeon
stoolie
suicide
suspect
suspicion
swag
swindle
syndicate
tail
tear gas
testify
testimony
theft
thief
trail
traitor
treason
trial

trigger
trooper
undercover
underworld
uniform
verdict
vice
victim
vigilante
villain
violate
violation
wanted
warden
warrant
watchdog
watchman
weapon
wire tap
witness
wound
writ
wrong
wrongdoing
yegg

Crime Phrases

A man is judged by the company he keeps . . . accessory after the fact . . . armed and extremely dangerous . . . armed to the teeth . . . ball and chain . . . behind bars . . . birds of a feather flock together . . . caught red-handed . . . chief of police . . . cloak and dagger . . . come clean . . . cop a plea . . . crack a safe . . . crime and punishment . . . crime does not pay . . . dead men

tell no tales . . . death house . . . death row . . . didn't
know it was loaded . . . elementary, my dear Watson .
. . escape artist . . . fire a shot . . . first degree murder
. . . first offense . . . Fu Manchu . . . hit and run . . .
hold for ransom . . . innocent 'till found guilty . . . Jack
the Ripper . . . jury of his peers . . . justice is blind . . .
kingpin . . . know right from wrong . . . law and order
. . . loan shark . . . machine gun . . . make the punishment fit the crime . . . make little ones out of big ones
. . . make my day . . . more than meets the FBI . . .
Mutiny on the Bounty . . . not guilty . . . out on parole
. . . out on bail . . . over the wall . . . perfect crime . . .
pin the rap on him . . . planted evidence . . . plead guilty
. . . pound of flesh . . . put the finger on him . . . read
'em their rights . . . rogue's gallery . . . scene of the
crime . . . Secret Service . . . serve a term . . . set a thief
to catch a thief . . . squad car . . . stick 'em up . . . strip-
ed suit . . . take him for a ride . . . take it on the lam .
. . ten most wanted list . . . the last mile . . . The Mir-
anda decision . . . third degree . . . trail by fury . . . two
wrongs don't make a right . . . undercover agent . . . up
the river . . . victimless crime . . . what do you hear from
the mob? . . . when a felon needs a friend.

Entry Example

STATEMENT: "I like (cleanser) because . . . like an
ace DETECTIVE, it TRAILS and never fails to make
the CRIMINAL dirt and greasy household grime COME
CLEAN quickly, safely, and economically."

DANCING

adagio
ball
ballerina
ballet
ballroom
band
beat
boogie-woogie
bossa nova
break
bunny hop
cakewalk
call
caller
Calypso
cha-cha
Charleston
choreography
chorus
clog
conga
couple
cue
cut in
dance
dance floor
dance hall
dancing
dip
discotheque
drag
duet
fandango
figure

follow
foot
fox trot
glide
hoedown
hoof
hop
hula
jam
jazz
jig
jitterbug
jukebox
kick
lead
limbo
lindy
mambo
march
May pole
meringue
minuet
movement
music
one-step
orchestra
partner
party
pirouette
pivot
play
polka
prance
prom

promenade
quadrille
ragtime
record
reel
rhythm
round
rumba
samba
saraband
shimmy
shuffle
slide
soft shoe
split
square
square dancing
stag
step
step-out
stomp
strut
sway
swing
swivel
syncopate
tag
tango
tap
tempo
tune
turn
twirl
twist

two-step   waltz
wall flower   whirl

Dancing Phrases

After the ball was over . . . Alexander's Ragtime Band . . . Anniversary Waltz . . . barn dance . . . Beer Barrel Polka . . . Big Apple . . . Black Bottom . . . bump and grind . . . change partners . . . cheek to cheek . . . conga line . . . Cotton-eyed Joe . . . cut a rug . . . dance of the seven veils . . . dancing bear . . . Dancing in the Dark . . . Darktown Strutters Ball . . . fan dance . . . follow-through . . . grand march . . . having a ball . . . highland fling . . . honor your partner . . . hoochy-coochy . . . I could dance all night . . . in the groove . . . light on your feet . . . Lindy Hop . . . may I have this dance? . . . on with the dance . . . pick your partner . . . put your best foot forward . . . rain dance . . . rock 'n' roll . . . rug cutter . . . shall we dance? . . . shuffle off to Buffalo . . . sit this one out . . . skip to my Lou . . . stompin' at the Savoy . . . swing your partner . . . takes two to tango . . . they're playing our song . . . three-quarter time . . . toe dance . . . trip the light fantastic . . . turkey trot . . . varsity drag . . . Virginia reel . . . waltz me around again, Willie . . . war dance . . . while the band played on.

Entry Example

I like (shampoo) because . . . I can just WALTZ through my wash with this active PARTNER that LEADS all others for "REEL" results at every STEP.

EDUCATION

ABC's
academy
accelerated
alumna
alumnus
bachelors
blackboard
campus
cap and gown
class
classic
classroom
coach
college
commence
  ment
course
cram
culture
curriculum
dean
degree
desk
diploma
doctorate
doctrine
dunce
educate
education
educational
egghead
elementary
enroll
examination

expel
expound
faculty
flunk
fraternity
freshman
grade
graduate
graduation
Greek
grind
higher
  education
homework
honors
information
initiate
institution
instruct
intellectual
interpret
junior
kindergarten
knowledge
learn
learning
lecture
lesson
magna cum
  laude
masters
mentor
monitor
mortar board

pass
pedagogue
Ph.D.
play hooky
postgraduate
practice
prep
professor
prom
promotion
pundit
pupil
sage
savant
scholar
scholarship
scholastic
school
schooling
schoolmate
secondary
senior
sheepskin
sophomore
sorority
student
study
subject
suspend
teach
teacher
teaching
term
test

textbook
theory
three R's
truant

tuition
tutor
undergraduate
university

vocational
wisdom
wise

Educational Phrases

Cut classes . . . English as a second language . . . go to the head of the class . . . knowledge is power . . . student of letters . . . master of arts . . . skip a grade . . . special education . . . you can lead students to college, but you can't make them think.

Entry Example

I prefer (ham) because . . . it EDUCATED my family's taste for better meat, TAUGHT us to appreciate first GRADE quality, and made (ham) our favorite COURSE.

Educational Entertainment

He's so stupid he thinks magna cum laude is a cloud formation.

ELECTRIC

AC
adapter
ampere
amplify
amps
appliance
arc
armature
attract
battery
beam
blow
blowout
bolt
bright
bulb
burn out
cable
candlepower
capacity
carry
chandelier
charge
circuit
circuit breaker
coil
condenser
conduct
conductor
connect
connection
consume
contact
convert

copper
cord
current
cut-out
cycle
DC
dim
discharge
disconnect
dry cell
dynamic
dynamo
electric
electrician
electricity
electrify
electrocute
engine
field
filament
fixture
flash
flow
fluctuate
fluorescent
force
frequency
fuse
galvanize
generate
generator
glare
glitter
globe

glow
grid
ground
heat
heater
hookup
illuminate
impulse
incandescent
induction
insulate
juice
kilowatt
lamp
light
lightning
line
lineman
load
luminous
magnet
meter
motor
negative
neon
nonconductor
ohm
oscillate
outlet
output
overload
phase
pickup
plug

pole	resistor	switch
positive	rheostat	tape
potential	shield	terminal
power	shine	transformer
powerhouse	shock	turbine
radiate	shocking	vacuum
ray	short	volt
rectify	socket	voltage
relay	solder	watt
remote control	spark	weld
repel	strand	wire
resistance	surge	wiring

Electrical Phrases

All lit up . . . alternating current . . . blackout . . .
blow a fuse . . . bolt from the blue . . . bright lights . . .
carry a current . . . current events . . . direct current . .
. electric chair . . . fuse box . . . heavy duty . . . high
frequency . . . high potential . . . high tension . . . high
voltage . . . indirect lighting . . . keep the wires hot . . .
know what's watt . . . let there be light . . . lightning
arrester . . . lightning rod . . . live wire . . . magnetic field
. . . nobody ohm . . . ohm on the range . . . peak load .
. . power plant . . . push button . . . short circuit . . . step
up the current . . . storage battery . . . third rail . . .
throw a switch . . . troubleshooter . . . turn off the
current.

Entry Example

I prefer (fruit) because . . . the delicious JUICE in
each golden GLOWING GLOBE has the POTENTIAL
to ELECTRIFY my family's breakfast appetite, GAL-
VANIZE our energy, and GENERATE good health.

EMPLOYMENT

action
advance
advancement
advertising
affirmative
application
apprentice
assistant
automation
avocation
beginner
benefits
blue collar
bonus
boss
breadwinner
brown-nosing
business
career
CEO
chief
civil service
commerce
commercial
company
compensation
concern
consultant
corporation
counseling
customer
dealer
department

desk
director
discharge
dismissal
domestic
drug testing
earn
earnings
education
employ
employee
employer
employment
executive
expert
factory
file
fire
firm
foreman
grind
handbooks
handicapped
help
help wanted
helper
hire
hired hand
idle
incentives
industrious
industry
interview

job
jobholder
labor
line
livelihood
loaf
man hour
management
manager
manned
manpower
manufacturer
merchant
morale
occupation
office politics
overtime
part-time
path
pay
payroll
perk
personnel
picket
piecework
pink slip
placement
plant
polygraph
president
production
profession
promote

promotion	shop	tool
qualify	sideline	trade
quit	situation	train
racket	specialist	transfer
raise	staff	tycoon
records	stock	union
rehabilitation	store	visas
relocation	strike	vocation
resume	superintendent	vocational
retire	supervise	wage
retrain	supervisor	white collar
salary	task	work
service	technical	worker
shift	testing	

Employment Phrases

A company is judged by the people it keeps . . . assembly line . . . board of directors . . . busy as a bee . . . busy as a one-armed paperhanger . . . child labor . . . daily grind . . . efficiency expert . . . employment agency . . . executive suite . . . get aboard . . . get the sack . . . hard labor . . . Heaven will protect the working girl . . . help wanted . . . hired hand . . . human resources development . . . jack of all trades . . . job seeker . . . learn a trade . . . learn while you earn . . . man-sized job . . . manual labor . . . meal ticket . . . mind your own business . . . on the job training . . . practice makes perfect . . . punch the clock . . . put on the payroll . . . roll up your sleeves . . . strike while the iron is hot . . . swing shift . . . time-and-a-half . . . what's my line? . . . work for peanuts . . . worth his salt.

Entry Example

(Watch brand) is the best choice for a watch because . . . with superior WORKS to keep it always on the JOB, it is dependable enough for a DOCTOR, precise enough for an ENGINEER, and rugged enough for a MINER.

FIRE AND HEAT

ablaze
afire
aflame
alarm
ardent
ardor
arson
asbestos
ashes
axe
bake
blast
blaze
blowtorch
boil
bonfire
brand
broil
burn
burner
caldron
candle
carbon
carbonize
cauterize
char
charcoal
chimney
cinder
clinker
coal
coke
combustible
combustion

conflagration
consume
cook
cremate
cremation
crisp
crucible
element
ember
engine
explode
extinguish
fagot
false alarm
fervent
fervor
fiery
fire
fire alarm
fire drill
fire engine
fire escape
fireball
firebug
firelight
fireman
fireplace
fireproof
fireworks
flame
flammable
flare
flue
forge

fry
fuel
furnace
fuse
gas
gas jet
glare
glow
grate
griddle
grill
hearth
heat
heater
hell
hellfire
holocaust
hose
hot
ignite
ignition
illuminate
incandescence
incendiary
incinerate
inferno
inflammable
kiln
kindle
kindling
lava
light
luminous
match

melt	scorch	swelter
molten	sear	taper
oil	seethe	thermal
oven	simmer	thermometer
overheat	singe	thermostat
phosphores-	sizzle	tinder
cent	slag	toast
poker	smelter	tongs
puff	smoke	torch
put out	smolder	torrid
pyre	snuff out	volcano
pyromaniac	spark	warm
radiate	steam	warmth
radiator	stoke	weld
range	stove	wildfire
red hot	strike	wood
roast	sultry	
scald	sun	

Fire and Heat Phrases

Add fuel to the fire . . . sparks fly . . . blow out the flame . . . brush fire . . . burned at the stake . . . burnt offering . . . burnt to a cinder . . . burst into flame . . . catch fire . . . feed the flames . . . flame thrower . . . flickering flames . . . four-alarm fire . . . glowing coals . . . heat wave . . . hook-and-ladder . . . hot as hell . . . make it hot for him . . . pluck a brand from the burning . . . pour oil on the flames . . . rake over the coals . . . rise like Phoenix from its ashes . . . set afire . . . smoke inhalation . . . Smokey the Bear . . . spontaneous combustion . . . strike a match . . . third degree burn . . . three-alarmer . . . where there's smoke, there's fire . . . white heat.

Entry Example

I like to lunch at (restaurant) because . . . for a LIGHT meal that STRIKES me just right, (restaurant's) food has no MATCH for wide RANGE and "GRATE" appeal.

Hot Gag

Loser: "Should I put more fire into my entries?"
Winner: "Better put more of your entries into the fire!"

FISHING

angler	fishy	perch
angling	flounder	pickerel
aquatic	fluke	pier
bait	fly	pike
barb	gaff	piscatory
basket	game	play
bass	gear	pole
bite	gill	pond
boat	goldfish	pool
bullhead	grunt	porpoise
calm	harpoon	ray
carp	hatch	reel
cast	hatchery	rise
catch	haul	river
catfish	herring	rod
caught	hook	roe
caviar	kingfish	sail
cod	lake	sailfish
crab	land	salmon
crawfish	lead	sardine
creek	leader	scale
creel	license	school
dive	line	sea
dock	lobster	seine
dolphin	lure	shad
drag	mackerel	shark
eel	marine	shoal
fin	minnow	shrimp
finny	mullet	sinker
fish	mussel	smelt
fish eggs	net	snapper
fisherman	ocean	snare
fishery	octopus	sole
fishing	oyster	spawn

spin	sunfish	tuna
spool	surf	wade
spoon	surface	water
stream	tackle	waves
strike	tide	whale
striper	trawl	whopper
sturgeon	troll	worms
sucker	trout	

Fishing Phrases

As much privacy as a goldfish . . . cast your line . . . catch of the day . . . denizen of the deep . . . drop a line . . . finny tribe . . . fish fry . . . fish in troubled waters . . . fish or cut bait . . . fish out of water . . . fish story . . . fisherman's luck . . . fishy business . . . flying fish . . . game fish . . . get a bite . . . gone fishing . . . hook, line and sinker . . . jelly fish . . . Jonah and the wale . . . land a big one . . . like living in a fish bowl . . . man eating shark . . . marine life . . . other fish to fry . . . pretty kettle of fish . . . prize catch . . . queer fish . . . red herring . . . rise to the bait . . . school of fish . . . sea food . . . swim upstream . . . thar she blows! . . . the one that got away.

Entry Example

I like to shop at (department store) because . . . when FISHING for a bargain, I get a WHALE of a deal from (department store's) complete LINE which always lets me NET a good buy.

FITNESS AND DIET

aerobics
backache
bicycling
bran
calories
center
cholesterol
chubby
curls
deprived
diet
exercise
exercise bike
fasting
fat
fiber
fitness
fruits
grains
gym
headband
health center

jogging
jump rope
lean
low fat
metabolism
minerals
muscles
natural
nonsmoker
nutrition
oats
obesity
overweight
physical
 fitness
portly
pull-ups
push-ups
rest
running
salt-free
sauna

sit-ups
slender
slim
stretching
supplements
svelte
swimming
thin
treadmill
trim
vegetables
vegetarian
vitamins
walking
water
weight
weight room
weights
whirlpool
yoga

Fitness and Diet Phrases

A la natural . . . diet is a four-letter word . . . fat as a pig . . . fat as a tub . . . hanging by a slender thread . . . lean 'n mean . . . oh, my aching back . . . rest stop . . . slim 'n trim . . . swimming in grease . . . that's really stretching it . . . thin as a rail.

Anonymous Quote

"This place requires no PHYSICAL FITNESS program. Everyone gets enough EXERCISE JUMPING to conclusions, flying off the handle, RUNNING down the boss, and dodging responsibility."

FOODS AND BEVERAGES

additives	cheese	dish
alcohol	chef	dough
ale	chemicals	drink
appetite	chew	eat
appetizer	chicken	edible
appetizing	chili	egg
applesauce	chop	entree
aroma	chow	epicure
bacon	cinnamon	ethnic
barbecue	clove	famine
batter	cocoa	famish
beans	coffee	fare
beef	coffee	fast
beer	confection	feast
beet	consume	feed
berry	cook	festive
beverage	cookbook	fish
biscuit	corn	flavor
bite	course	flesh
bologna	cracker	flour
bread	cream	food
breakfast	crust	fowl
broth	cuisine	fresh
bun	cup	frosting
butter	currant	fruit
cabbage	curry	fry
cake	dairy	garlic
calorie	date	garnish
can	dessert	ginger
canape	devour	gorge
candy	diet	gourmet
carrot	digest	grain
celery	dine	gravy
cereal	dinner	grill

grocery	mustard	recipe
grub	nightcap	relish
gruel	noodle	restaurant
gum	nourish	rice
ham	nourishment	roast
hamburger	nut	roll
hash	nutrition	rye
herb	nutritious	sage
hominy	oatmeal	salad
hot dog	oats	salt
hunger	onion	sandwich
hungry	oven	sauce
ice cream	overeat	sausage
jam	pancake	savor
jelly	pantry	season
juice	pasta	seasoning
ketchup	pastry	seconds
kettle	peach	serve
kitchen	pear	shortening
knife	pepper	simmer
kosher	pickle	snack
lamb	pie	soda
lard	pizza	soda pop
larder	plum	soup
lemon	pop	spice
lettuce	porridge	spinach
loaf	potato	spread
lunch	potluck	starch
mayonnaise	poultry	starve
meal	preserve	steak
meat	provision	stew
menu	prune	stir
mild	pudding	stomach
mint	punch	stove
mix	raisin	stuffing
morsel	range	sugar
mouth	raspberry	sup
mushroom	ration	supper

swallow	toast	vodka
syrup	tomato	waffle
table	tongue	waiter
taco	tripe	wheat
tamale	turkey	whiskey
tea	vegetable	wine
thirst	victuals	yeast
thyme	vinegar	
tidbit	vitamin	

Food and Beverage Phrases

Add a dash of spice . . . apple of their eye . . . balanced meal . . . banana oil . . . big cheese . . . bill of fare . . . bring home the bacon . . . can't stomach that . . . chicken feed . . . chuck wagon . . . come and get it . . . cooking with gas . . . cream of the crop . . . dinner bell . . . drop it like a hot potato . . . easy as pie . . . eat, drink and be merry . . . family style . . . fat's in the fire . . . fed up . . . feeling my oats . . . food for thought . . . from soup to nuts . . . get on the gravy train . . . give the raspberry . . . gone to pot . . . good provider . . . good to the last drop . . . got a lot of crust . . . hard-boiled egg . . . home cooking . . . in a pickle . . . in a stew . . . just "desserts" . . . love at first bite . . . main course . . . meal ticket . . . midnight snack . . . not by bread alone . . . not my cup of tea . . . not worth their salt . . . nouvelle cuisine . . . one person's meat is another's poison . . . raid the refrigerator . . . slow as molasses . . . small potatoes . . . solid food . . . sour grapes . . . spill the beans . . . square meal . . . staff of life . . . stick to the ribs . . . talk turkey . . . toast of the town . . . water, water everywhere, but not a drop to drink . . . well done . . . what foods these morsels be!

Entry Example

A vacation in (seaside resort) would be . . . SPICED with fishing sprees, SEASONED with sensational sights, STIRRED with SALT air, BAKED with sunshine, and SERVED with pleasure.

Fun Fare

Honeymoon dish: just lettuce alone . . . No matter how young a prune may be, it's always full of wrinkles . . . When he beefed about the cold ham, his wife gave him some hot tongue . . . When the judge is eating sirloin, would you say His Honor is at steak?

"What did the egg say in the monastery?"
"Out of the frying pan, into the friar!"

A drunk was brought into court. When he appeared before the Judge, his honor said, "I understand you're here for drinking."
And the drunk replied "I'm ready if you are!"

FOOTBALL

All-American
anchor
attack
back
backfield
ball
beat
bench
block
boot
bowl game
buck
captain
carry
catch
center
champion
championship
charge
cheer
coach
college
cornerback
cover
crossbar
crossover
defeat
defense
defensive
down
drawback
drill
dropkick
eleven

end
end run
end zone
evade
extra point
fake
fan
feint
field
field goal
flank
football
formation
forward
fullback
fumble
gain
game
goal
goal line
goal posts
grid
gridiron
guard
half
halfback
helmet
holding
huddle
instant replay
intercept
interference
key player
kick

kick off
line
line-up
lineman
lose
loss
muff
offense
offensive
offside
opening
opponent
oval
overtime
pass
penalty
pigskin
pile up
pivot
play
player
playoff
pocket
point
position
post
practice
pro
protect
punt
quarter
quarterback
rally
receive

recover	signal	throw
referee	snap	tie
regular	spin	time out
reverse	spiral	touchdown
root	sport	train
rules	sprint	uniform
run	squad	varsity
rush	station	victory
safety	strategy	wedge
score	substitute	win
scout	super bowl	wing
scrimmage	switch	wishbone
shift	tackle	yard
shotgun	team	yardage
sideline	team mate	zigzag
sidestep	teamwork	

Football Phrases

All-American team . . . ball carrier . . . block that kick
. . . broken field runner . . . buck the line . . . call the
play . . . call signals . . . carry the ball . . . cheer leader
. . . cheering section . . . clear field ahead . . . complete
a pass . . . defensive play . . . drop the ball . . . even the
score . . . final quarter . . . first down . . . first team . .
. flying wedge . . . forward pass . . . hit the line . . . hold
that line . . . Ivy League . . . line plunge long run . . . out
of bounds . . . pass the ball . . . quarterback draw . . .
run interference . . . scoreless tie . . . second team . . .
skull practice . . . steam roller . . . stiff arm . . . throw for
a loss . . . tote the leather . . . triple threat . . . wide
open.

Statement Example

When mother's GOAL is family health, she TACK-LES vitamin lack by serving whole wheat bread, SCOR-ING a TOUCHDOWN with UNIFORM nourishment in the food FIELD.

Limerick Lingo

To college Dad sent his son, Jack
Paying bills every year by the stack.
Now what can Dad show
For spending that dough?
All he got was a lone QUARTER BACK!

GARDENING AND PLANTS

annuals
apple
arbor
ash
aster
atrium
bean
bean pole
bed
bedding plant
beech
beet
berry
birch
blight
bloom
blossom
bonsai
botany
bough
bounty
branch
bud
bulb
burr
bush
buttercup
cabbage
cactus
canal
cane
care
carnation
carrot

cedar
chaff
charcoal
cherry
chestnut
clover
cold frame
compost
coniferous
corn
cotton
creeper
crocus
crop
cross
cucumber
cultivate
culture
daffodil
daisy
dandelion
date
deciduous
dig
dirt
drainage
earth
edible
elm
evergreen
fence
fertile
fertilize
field

fig
fir
floral
flower
flowerpot
flowers
foliage
forest
frames
fresh
frost
fruit
furrow
garden
gardener
germinate
gloves
graft
grain
grass
greenery
greenhouse
greens
ground
grove
grow
growth
hanging basket
harvest
hazel
hedge
hemlock
herb
hickory

hoe
holly
hops
horticulture
hose
hothouse
house plant
humus
hybrid
hydroponics
irrigate
ivy
kernel
landscape
laurel
lawn
lawn mower
leaf
lettuce
lilac
lily
lime
loam
maize
manure
maple
meadow
melon
mint
mock
mow
mower
mulberry
mulch
nursery
nut
oak
oats

olive
orchard
orchid
organic
packet
pansy
parsley
pea
peach
peanut
pear
peat
pecan
peony
perennial
petunia
pine
plant
plants
plot
plow
plum
pod
poison ivy
pollen
pollinate
poplar
poppy
potato
potting soil
primrose
prune
ragweed
rain
raise
raisin
rake
reap

ripe
rocky
root
root cellar
rose
rototiller
row
rye
sage
sand
sap
sapling
season
seed
seedling
shamrock
shrub
smudge pot
sod
soil
sow
spade
spray
sprinkler
sprout
spruce
squash
stalk
stem
sun
sycamore
tansy
thistle
thorn
thyme
till
timothy
tomato

transplant	variety	wheat
tree	vase	wheelbarrow
trellis	vegetable	willow
trowel	vine	window box
tuber	violet	wintergreen
tulip	walnut	woods
tumbleweed	water	yew
turf	watering can	yield
twig	weed	zinnia

Gardening and Plant Phrases

Apple of my eye . . . as alike as peas in a pod . . . as ye sow, so shall ye reap . . . can't see the forest for the trees . . . clinging vine . . . common garden variety . . . cool as a cucumber . . . cream of the crop . . . gone to seed . . . grow wild . . . know your oats . . . raise cane . . . separate the wheat from the chaff . . . rain forest . . . sow wild oats . . . this is the forest primeval . . . weeping willow.

Entry Example

I favor (President's name) for President because— he'll PLOW UNDER communistic WEEDS, PLANT SEEDS of honest government, CULTIVATE individual liberty, REAP a wholesome American HARVEST.

GEOGRAPHY

acre
altitude
archeological
area
belt
caves
city
compass
creek
dale
dell
desert
district
East
equator
field
forest
fork
formation
geography
geological
gully

hemisphere
hill
hollow
lake
latitude
longitude
map
meadow
mesa
mountain
municipality
North
ocean
parish
peak
plain
plateau
plot
precinct
quarter
region
ridge

river
road
rural
sea
section
sector
South
stratosphere
stream
territory
town
tract
tunnel
urban
valley
volcano
ward
West
woods
zone

Geographical Phrases

As old as the hills . . . babe in the woods . . . city slicker . . . East is East and West is West . . . fork over . . . head for the hills . . . make a mountain out of a molehill . . . not worth a hill of beans . . . over hill and dale . . . plain and simple . . . stream of consciousness . . . take a peak . . . take the high road . . . the plot thickens.

Wee Wisdom

"What's the difference between history and geography?" the teacher asked her pupil. "Geography tells me where I am—history tells me how I got there."

GEOLOGY, ROCKS AND MINERALS

age	gold	pearl
anthracite	granite	phosphorus
basalt	graphite	pillar
base rock	imitation	quarry
bituminous	inorganic	quartz
brilliance	iron	range
carbon	jewelry	rarity
carbon-date	karat	reef
color	lava	salt
copper	lime	sandstone
crust	magma	shaft
crystal	marble	shale
cutting	mesa	shelf
diamond	metal	silver
durability	metals	stalactite
element	millimeters	stalagmite
epoch	mine	stone
era	molten	synthetic
erosion	moraine	transparency
formation	natural	uplift
gemstones	nitrate	volcanic
geode	nuggets	
glacier	ore	

Geology, Rock and Mineral Phrases

A person of color . . . act your age . . . color me gone . . . diamond in the rough . . . every cloud has a silver lining . . . gold digger . . . heavy metal . . . only a stone's throw away . . . pearls of wisdom . . . salt of the earth . . . short shelf life . . . silver fox . . . upper crust.

Fictional Characterization

His face was etched with the EROSION of many years. Gray had almost overtaken his COPPER hair. While his arms were no longer MARBLED with rippling muscles, there was still an aura of strength about him. Even before he spoke, you sensed this was a man of IRON. When he began to address the crowd, his words were as hot and flowing as MOLTEN LAVA.

GOLF

ace	fore	range
address	foursome	roll
amateur	game	rough
approach	golf	round
backswing	golfer	sand trap
bad lie	grass	score
bag	green	scratch
ball	grip	shaft
birdie	handicap	shank
bogey	hazard	shot
brassie	hit	sinker
bunker	hole	slice
caddie	hook	spoon
cart	iron	stance
chip	lie	stick
club	links	stroke
clubhouse	loft	swing
course	lose	tee
cup	match	tee off
distance	match play	tie
divot	miniature	trap
drive	novice	turf
driver	obstacle	twosome
dub	par	wedge
duffer	play	win
eagle	pro	wood
fairway	putt	
flag	putter	

Golf Phrases

Above par . . . address the ball . . . below par . . .
break a hundred . . . cry or yell "fore!" . . . divot digger

. . . driving iron . . . eighteen holes . . . finish in the money . . . follow through . . . hole in one . . . in the groove . . . in the rough . . . incoming nine . . . keep your eyes on the ball . . . long drive . . . lost ball . . . miniature golf . . . miss the ball . . . nine holes . . . Nineteenth Hole . . . open championship . . . outgoing nine . . . over par . . . par for the course . . . play through . . . practice shot . . . shoot a birdie . . . sink the ball . . . square the hole . . . tee shot . . . trick shot . . . under par . . . up to par . . . utility club . . . water hazard.

Entry Example

I like (coffee) because . . . when daily chores PUTT me in the ROUGH, a steaming CUP of (coffee) DRIVES away weariness at one STROKE, pepping me up for another ROUND.

HORSE RACING

ahead
backstretch
bareback
barrier
bay
beat
best bet
bet
bit
blaze
blinkers
bookie
bookmaker
boot
break
bred
breed
breeze
bridle
canter
chariot
cinch
claim
clock
colors
colt
course
dam
derby
dismount
distance
dope
dopester
driver

entry
equine
fan
fast
favorite
field
filly
finish
first
fleet
foal
form
front
furlong
Futurity
gait
gallop
gate
girth
grandstand
groom
handicap
harness
hay
heels
homestretch
hoof
horse
hot tip
hurdle
jockey
judge
lap
lead

length
lineage
lope
lose
maiden
mane
mare
marking
mount
mudder
nag
neck
neigh
nicker
nose
oats
odds
oval
overtake
owner
pace
paddock
parimutuel
parlay
pay off
pedigree
place
plug
pony
pool
position
post
potential
purse

quirt	speed	threat
race	sport	thoroughbred
racehorse	spur	ticket
raceway	stable	tie
racing	stakes	tip
rail	stall	tout
rein	stallion	track
result	stand	train
ride	start	trot
rider	starter	turf
roan	steed	upset
run	steeplechase	wager
saddle	steward	weight
scratch	stirrup	whinny
season	straightaway	whip
selector	stretch	win
shod	stride	winner
shoe	stud	wire
show	sulky	workout
silks	sweepstakes	yearling
sire	swift	
sleeper	tail	

Horse Racing Phrases

Across the board . . . also ran . . . big ticket . . . bum steer . . . coming down the stretch . . . daily double . . . dark horse . . . dead heat . . . dope sheet . . . fast track . . . finish line . . . finish strong . . . fix a race . . . front runner . . . gain ground . . . hay burner . . . hobby horse . . . hold the pace . . . horse and buggy . . . horse around . . . horse laugh . . . horse sense . . . improve the breed . . . in the money . . . Kentucky Derby . . . King of Sports . . . knows his oats . . . lengths in front . . . long shot . . . Man o' War . . . neck and neck . . . oat burner . . . odds-on favorite . . . on the right track . . . pace setter . . . past performance . . . peak performance . . .

photo finish . . . play the ponies . . . racing form . . . racing season . . . riding habit . . . show his heels . . . slow track . . . start fast . . . starting gate . . . straight from the horse's mouth . . . sure thing . . . sure winner . . . take a hurdle . . . take a spill . . . Triple Crown . . . turn out to pasture . . . Twenty Grand . . . under the wire . . . victory wreath . . . win by a nose . . . win in a walk . . . win, place or show . . . winners circle . . . winning streak . . . winning ticket.

Entry Example

I like to save at (bank) because . . . in the RACE for security, my money is on the right TRACK here, where interest STARTS FAST, holds the PACE, and PAYS OFF big!

HUNTING

aim	dog	kill
ammunition	draw	lance
animal	duck	leopard
archer	elk	let fly
arms	escape	license
arrow	falcon	limit
at bay	field	lion
badger	fire	load
bag	firearm	lynx
bait	flee	marksman
bay	flight	moose
beagle	flush	net
bear	footprint	outdoors
bearer	forest	pack
beast	fox	panther
bird	fur	pellet
blind	game	pelt
bloodhound	gauge	pheasant
boar	gear	pierce
boomerang	goose	pistol
bow	grouse	pointer
buck	guide	pounce
buckshot	gun	preserve
bullet	hare	prey
caliber	hawk	print
camouflage	hide	puma
capture	hit	quail
cartridge	horn	quarry
catch	hound	quiver
charge	hunt	rabbit
chase	hunter	range
clip	hunting	reindeer
decoy	huntress	retrieve
deer	jungle	rifle

rifleman	spoor	trophy
safari	sport	tusk
scent	stalk	varmint
season	target	warden
shell	tiger	weapon
shoot	track	wild
shot	trail	wilderness
shotgun	trap	wildlife
sight	trapper	wolf
slay	tree	woods
snare	treed	
spear	trigger	

Hunting Phrases

Big game hunter . . . bird dog . . . bow and arrow . . . bring 'em back alive . . . bring home the bacon . . . buck fever . . . call of the wild . . . draw a bead . . . fluorescent orange . . . follow a scent . . . good hunting! . . . Great White Hunter . . . Happy Hunting Ground . . . hot on the trail . . . loaded for bear . . . lose the scent . . . on the wing . . . open season . . . out of season . . . out on a limb . . . play possum . . . pull the trigger . . . ride to hounds . . . rough it . . . set a trap . . . small game . . . trap line . . . wild goose chase . . . within range.

Entry Example

I shop at (grocery store) because . . . when HUNTING for food bargains, I always find high CALIBER products in the BAG at a price RANGE that's lowest in the FIELD.

INDIANS

adobe	Indian	sannup
ambush	knife	savage
arrow	lance	scalp
attack	lodge	shaman
bareback	long house	spear
barter	maize	squaw
bison	massacre	taboo
blanket	migrate	tent
bonnet	moccasin	tepee
bow	moon	territory
brave	mustang	tomahawk
buck	native	totem
buffalo	nomad	totem pole
calumet	paddle	track
camp	paint	trade
canoe	paleface	trail
ceremony	papoose	treaty
chief	peace pipe	tribal
chieftain	plain	tribe
clan	pony	wampum
council	powwow	war bonnet
dugout	primitive	war cry
feather	pueblo	war dance
firewater	raid	war paint
forest	red man	warrior
guide	redskin	wickiup
half-breed	reservation	wigwam
headdress	sachem	wild
hunter	sacrifice	

Indian Phrases

Burial ground . . . burn at the stake . . . by the shores of Gitchee Gummee . . . cliff dweller . . . cowboys and Indians . . . feather in his bonnet . . . Great White Father . . . Happy Hunting Grounds . . . heap big chief . . . hi ho, Silver . . . Indian Love Call . . . Indian maid . . . Indian summer . . . last of the Mohicans . . . Lo, the poor Indian! . . . all chiefs and no Indians . . . noble redskin . . . noble savage . . . on the warpath . . . rain dance . . . rain god . . . Rain-in-the-face . . . sell Manhattan Island for $24 . . . Sitting Bull . . . smoke the peace pipe . . . smoke signal . . . snake dance . . . sun dancer . . . sun worship . . . ten little Indians . . . the Vanishing American . . . this is the forest primeval . . . war whoop . . . way down yonder in the Indian nation . . . where the deer and the antelope play.

Entry Example

I like to deal with my (neighborhood grocer) because . . . he never tries to SCALP me with high prices, gives real value for every BUCK without RESERVATION, and delivers orders so I needn't TOTEM.

INSECTS

ant
antenna
bee
beetles
body parts
bug
bumblebee
butterfly
centipede
cockroach
cocoon
colony
crawl
creepy
dragon fly
eerie
entomology
exterminator

firefly
fly
grasshopper
gypsie moths
head
hill
hive
hornet
infest
intimidating
kill
lady bugs
larva
legs
locust
menacing
millipede
mosquito

moth
pest
queen
roach
scary
slugs
spider
squish
stink bug
swarm
tarantula
wasp
water skippers
web
weird
worker
worm

Insect Phrases

Crawl before you can walk . . . don't bug me . . . he makes me feel creepy . . . I'd kill for that dress . . . it's a fly by night outfit . . . Oh, what a tangled web we weave, when first we practice to deceive! . . . you won't worm your way out of this one.

Slogan

She's got L'eggs.

Insect Insanity

My son's fifth grade class just conducted a science experiment which proved sex doesn't exist. They put a bird and a bee in a cage together . . . and nothing happened.

INSURANCE

adjustable life
agent
annuity
beneficiary
business
car
cash value
collision
complete
comprehensive
contents
contract
cost index
coverage
deductible
discount

dividend
double
  indemnity
exclusion
extensive
face amount
fire
flood
grace period
health
home
insurance
insured
lapsed
liability
life

limits
paid-up
insurance
policy
protection
reinstatement
representative
rider
security
term
theft
underwriting
waiver
whole life

Insurance Phrases

Against our policy . . . circuit rider . . . full term body
. . . home is where the heart is . . . life is just a bowl of
cherries . . . none of your business . . . oh, give me a
home where the buffalo roam . . . prenuptial contract
. . . secret agent . . . that's off limits.

Entry Example

Our (burgler alarm) will give you a sense of SECU-
RITY. It will keep criminals OFF-LIMITS, keep your
HOME safe, and make your LIFE a lot more relaxed.

LEGAL

accessory
accuse
acquit
acquittal
action
adjournment
administer
administrator
advocate
affidavit
affirm
alibi
alimony
allege
appeal
appear
appearance
apprehend
argue
argument
arraign
arrest
attach
attachment
attorney
authority
bail
bail bond
bailiff
bankruptcy
bar
barrister
behest
bench

bench warrant
bequeath
bequest
bill
blue law
bond
brief
calendar
case
challenge
charge
circumstantial
  evidence
clemency
client
co-respondent
commit
commutation
commute
complainant
complaint
concurrent
confess
confession
consecutive
consent
contempt
conveyance
convict
conviction
cop
corporate
corpus delicti
counsel

counsellor
court
court order
crime
cross-examine
cross
  examination
custody
damages
decide
decision
decree
deed
defend
defendant
defender
defense
deputize
deputy
detain
discharge
dismiss
district
  attorney
divorce
document
double jeop-
  ardy
enforce
equity
escrow
estate
evict
evidence

examine
execute
executor
extradite
felony
first-degree
free
garnish
grand jury
guilty
habeas corpus
hear
hearing
hold
homicide
hostile
illegal
imprison
indict
indictment
inform
injunction
inquest
intent
jail
judge
judgment
judicial
jurist
juror
jury
justice
law
lawbreaker
lawful
lawless
lawsuit

lawyer
legacy
legal
liable
libel
liberty
litigate
litigation
magistrate
malice
manslaughter
martial
matron
misdemeanor
mistrial
motion
mouthpiece
oath
objection
offender
offense
opinion
order
ordinance
panel
pardon
parole
perjury
plaintiff
plea
plead
police
presentiment
prison
prisoner
proceeding
prohibit

prosecute
prosecution
prosecutor
quash
referee
regulation
reprieve
respondent
restrain
restraining
  order
retainer
reversal
reverse
right
ruling
separation
sheriff
shyster
slander
stand
statute
subpoena
sue
suit
summons
swear
talesman
testament
testify
testimony
trial
trustee
try
venire
venue
verdict

warrant	witness
will	writ

Legal Phrases

Bar of justice . . . bear witness . . . before the court . . . before the fact . . . Bill of Rights . . . bring false witness . . . case dismissed . . . caught in the act . . . cause for action . . . cease and desist . . . change of venue . . . contempt of court . . . court of last resort . . . directed verdict . . . drop a case . . . due process of law . . . fair trial . . . false witness . . . grounds for suit . . . hearsay evidence . . . higher court . . . His Honor . . . hold for trial . . . hold in contempt . . . holding cell . . . it's the law . . . John Doe . . . jury of his peers . . . justice of the peace . . . last will and testament . . . leading the witness . . . long arm of the law . . . lower court . . . material witness . . . no contest . . . not guilty . . . objection overruled . . . objection sustained . . . opposing counsel . . . order in the court . . . plead guilty . . . post a bond . . . power of attorney . . . reverse a decision . . . scales of justice . . . sealed verdict . . . set free . . . settle out of court . . . strike from the record . . . Supreme Court . . . take the stand . . . the people . . . the truth, the whole truth, and nothing but the truth . . . trial by jury . . . true bill . . . try a case . . . turn State's evidence . . . twelve good men and true . . . under oath . . . uphold the law . . . waive his rights . . . we, the jury . . . where there's a will, there's a lawyer . . . win a case . . . without bail.

Entry Example

From actual TRIAL, I can TESTIFY that this product always wins my family's VERDICT of approval, giving EVIDENCE of its worth.

LOVE AND MARRIAGE

adore
adultery
aisle
alter
amour
anniversary
annulment
attendant
bachelor
behavior
bells
best man
betroth
betrothal
bigamy
bouquet
breadwinner
bridal
bride
bridegroom
bridesmaid
carat
ceremony
cherish
church
clergyman
clinch
communication
compatibility
confetti
congratulations
counseling
couple
court

courtship
custom
darling
date
diamond
divorce
domestic
domestic
  relations
double wed-
  ding
dowry
elope
engage
engagement
escort
ethics
family
festive
fiancee
flirt
flowers
formal dress
friendship
gift
go steady
gown
groom
honeymoon
hope chest
hubby
husband
I do
in-laws

invitation
jilt
kiss
license
love
lover
marital
marriage
marriage
  license
marry
match
matchmaker
mate
matrimonial
matrimony
minister
newlyweds
nuptial
offspring
old maid
parson
present
priest
proposal
propose
rabbi
reception
rehearsal
relations
relationship
rice
ring
ring bearer

rites
romance
romantic
sentimental
separate
service
sex
shower
significant
  other
single
spark
spinster

spouse
squire
suitor
support
swain
sweetheart
therapy
toast
train
trousseau
unmarried
usher
veil

vow
wed
wedding
wedding band
wedding gown
wedding march
wedding party
wedding rites
wedlock
wife
witness
woo

Love and Marriage Phrases

All the world loves a lover . . . ask for her hand . . . bachelor dinner . . . ball and chain . . . bells are ringing . . . better half . . . bill and coo . . . bonds of matrimony . . . boy meets girl . . . bride and groom . . . broken engagement . . . catered affair . . . civil ceremony . . . come on, be a support . . . confirmed bachelor . . . cut the cake . . . Dear John letter . . . do you take this woman? . . . eternal triangle . . . fall in love . . . father-in-law . . . father's consent . . . flower girl . . . forever hold your peace . . . get spliced . . . give away the bride . . . going together . . . grounds for divorce . . . heir-conditioned . . . here comes the bride . . . just married . . . justice of the peace . . . keep company . . . kiss the bride . . . lawful wedded wife . . . left waiting at the church . . . love affair . . . love and kisses . . . love, honor and obey . . . love letter . . . lovers' lane . . . maid of honor . . . maiden name . . . man and wife . . . marry-go-round . . . mating season . . . May and December . . . members of the wedding . . . mother-in-law . . . Mr. and Mrs . . . .never the twain shall meet . . . old flame . . . perfect match . . . prenuptial contract . . . pop the question . . . ring the belle . . . take his name . . . the urge to merge . . . three little words . . . throw rice (or old shoes) . . . tie the knot . . . ties that bind . . . sea of matrimony . . . shotgun marriage . . . son and heir . . . support in accustomed style . . . until death do us part . . . wedding bliss . . . wedding bells . . . wedding guest . . . who's the lucky fellow? . . . yes, sir, that's by baby!

Entry Example

I prefer (syrup) because . . . WEDDING real butter and maple flavor in a perfect MARRIAGE, its ENGAGING taste has no MATCH for pleasing the "BEST MAN" in my house.

Love Laughs

Every woman should be in love with an archeologist; as you get older, he gets more interested.

Nothing in skirts is safe around him. But the other day he met a Scotsman. The guy almost killed him.

MAGIC AND MYSTIC

abracadabra
amaze
amulet
apparition
appearance
astonish
astrology
augur
aura
awe
bat
bewitch
beyond
bizarre
black magic
blanch
bogy
channel
charm
clairvoyance
coffin
conjure
conjuror
coven
creepy
crystal ball
cult
curse
deceive
deception
delusion
demon
destiny
devil

disappear
divine
dragon
eerie
enchant
escape
ESP
evoke
exorcise
extrasensory
  perception
fairy
fakir
fantasy
fetish
flying saucer
force
forecast
foretell
formula
fortune
fortune teller
frighten
future
genie
ghastly
ghost
gnome
goblin
gooseflesh
grave
gremlin
grisly
gruesome

gypsy
Halloween
hallucination
haunt
haunting
hereafter
hex
hobgoblin
hoodoo
horoscope
horrify
horror
Houdini
hypnotize
idol
illusion
image
incantation
influence
invisible
invoke
jinn
jinx
legend
legerdemain
lore
Lucifer
luck
magic
magician
marvel
marvelous
medicine man
medium

mental	puzzle	supernatural
mesmerize	quake	supernormal
mind reader	queer	symbol
miracle	reading	taboo
mirage	riddle	talisman
monster	rite	telepathy
mysterious	Satan	terrify
mystery	scare	terror
mystic	seance	tomb
mystify	secret	trance
myth	seer	trick
necromancy	seeress	uncanny
obsession	shiver	unearthly
occult	shock	unknown
odd	shudder	unseen
omen	sign	unusual
oracle	skeleton	vampire
pale	soothsayer	vanish
palm reader	sorcerer	vision
phantom	sorceress	visitation
phenomena	sorcery	voodoo
philter	specter	wand
possessed	spectral	weird
possession	spell	wide-eyed
potion	spellbound	wish
powder	sphinx	witch
predict	spirit	witchcraft
prediction	spook	wizard
prestidigitator	sprite	wonder
prophecy	startle	wraith
prophet	strange	yoga
psychic	superman	zombie

Magic and Mystic Phrases

Abominable Snowman . . . bell, book and candle . .
. black cat . . . cast a spell . . . cloak of invisibility . . .

crystal ball or globe . . . Dame Fortune . . . divining rod
. . . evil eye . . . evil spirit . . . fairy tale . . . fly on a
broomstick . . . gaze into the crystal . . . good fairy . . .
gruesome twosome . . . guardian angel . . . haunted
house . . . hocus pocus . . . Indian rope trick . . . inner
sanctum . . . Lady Luck . . . magic circle . . . magic lamp
. . . magic ring . . . magic wand . . . make your flesh
creep . . . Midas touch . . . mind over matter . . . more
things in heaven and earth . . . mumbo jumbo . . . nothing up his sleeve . . . now you see it, now you don't . .
. open sesame . . . other world . . . ouija board . . . out
of this world . . . Pandora's box . . . presto chango! . .
. pull a rabbit out of a hat . . . put a curse on . . . reading tea leaves . . . rub Aladdin's lamp . . . saw a person
in half . . . second sight . . . sleight of hand . . . spirit
world . . . strange but true . . . take a card—any card .
. . the hand is quicker than the eye . . . things that go
bump in the night . . . thought wave . . . three wishes .
. . truth is stranger than fiction . . . turn pale . . . twilight
zone . . . under a spell . . . unidentified flying objects .
. . vanishing act . . . wave a wand . . . wishing cap . . .
wishing well . . . witches' brew or cauldron . . . when the
spirit moves one . . . whirling dervish . . . white magic .
. . white witch . . . you're in my power.

Entry Example

I like (soap) because . . . it makes cleaning an easy
TRICK, causes stains to VANISH, dirt to DISAPPEAR,
and brings ENCHANTING brightness to everything
touched by its MAGIC WAND.

MARINE AND OCEAN

barnacle
beach
beacon
bends
boat
buoy
canal reef
clam
coral
crab
crayfish
current
dive
diving bell
dolphin
eel
fish
hermit crab
high tide
islands
jellyfish

killer whale
lighthouse
lobster
low tide
marine
mermaid
muscle
ocean
octopus
oyster
pier
plants
reef
riptide
salt
sand
sand dollar
sea
sea horse
sea urchin
seashore

shale
shark
ship
shrimp
squid
starfish
stingray
submarine
surf
swell
swim
tide
tide pool
turtle
undertow
volcano
waiting
wave
whale
wharf
whitecap

Marine and Ocean Phrases

A whale of a time . . . currents run deep . . . don't
wait for your ship to come in, sail out to it . . . gone
fishin' . . . he clams up around her . . . like a fish out of
water . . . salt your mailing list . . . surf 'n turf . . . take
a dive.

Fictional Characterization

Lisa was a woman of contrasts. Possessed with the exuberance of roaring SURF, she could also be moody and vicious. A harmless STARFISH one day; a dangerous STINGRAY the next. Around her he often felt BEACHED--as helpless as a WHALE stranded at LOW TIDE.

MATHEMATICS

account
acre
add
addition
algebra
amount
angle
arc
area
arithmetic
breadth
bushel
calculate
calculus
cancel
carry
century
cipher
circle
circumference
compute
count
cube
cubic
curve
day
decade
decimal
decrease
degree
denominator
depth
diagram
diameter

digit
dimension
divide
division
double
dozen
economics
equal
equation
example
factor
figure
first
foot
formula
fraction
gallon
geometry
gram
grand
graph
half
halve
height
high
hour
hundred
inch
increase
length
linear
long
math
mathematics

measure
meter
mile
million
minus
minute
multiple
multiplication
multiply
number
numeral
oblong
ounce
peck
percentage
pi
pint
plane
plus
pound
power
probabilities
problem
quantity
quotient
radius
reckon
rectangle
reduce
remainder
result
rod
root
scale

sequence
single
slide rule
solution
solve
sphere
square
square root
statistics
subtract
subtraction

sum
tally
theorem
thousand
thrice
times table
ton
total
triangle
trigonometry
triple

triplet
twice
twin
unit
volume
whole
width
yard
zero

Mathematical Phrases

Baker's dozen . . . common denominator . . .divide and conquer . . . figures never lie . . . fourth dimension . . . go like sixty . . . high, wide and handsome . . . higher mathematics . . . his number is up . . . law of averages . . . never the twain shall meet . . . reading, writing and 'rithmetic . . . right angle . . . sum it up . . . to the nth degree . . . two pints make one cavort.

Entry Examples

I like (coupons) because . . . there's a PECK of fun selecting merchandise gifts from BUSHELS of prize premiums, but never an OUNCE of regret for top-quality products bought.

I prefer (cleanser) because . . . its speedy grease-foe ingredients DOUBLES my leisure by HALVING my cleaning time, while friendly (cleanser) ADDS protection to surfaces and hands by SUBTRACTING roughness.

MEASUREMENTS

acre	height	pint
barrel	inch	pound
bushel	kilogram	quart
centimeter	kilometer	quarter
circumference	knot	radius
cup	length	rod
diameter	liter	ruler
eighth	meter	score
foot	mile	section
furlong	milligram	tablespoon
gallon	millimeter	teaspoon
gram	ounce	whole
group	peck	width
half	perimeter	yard
hectare	pi	yardstick

Measurements Phrases

Did you score . . . give her an inch and she'll take a foot . . . goes a mile a minute . . . half a loaf is better than none . . . my cup runneth over . . . north forty . . .pound of flesh . . . put your foot in your mouth . . . she/he is a barrel of fun . . . spare the rod, spoil the child . . . the meter is running . . . tie the knot . . . yard sale.

Slogan
(for rope manufacturer)

We go to great LENGTHS KNOT to disappoint you.

MEDICAL AND HEALTH

accident
ache
acupressure
acupuncture
acute
addict
administer
ail
ailment
allergic
allergy
ambulance
anatomy
anesthetic
antidote
antiseptic
artery
attending
autopsy
back
bacteria
bag
bandage
bed
benign
birth
birthmark
bleed
blind
blood
board-certified
bodily
body
brain

breath
breathe
bruise
caduceus
capsule
care
case
cast
cell
chart
checkup
chemotherapy
chew
chiropractor
chronic
circulation
clinic
coma
complaint
confine
consultation
contagious
corpsman
cough
cramp
curable
cure
dead
deaf
death
dental
dentist
diagnose
diagnosis

die
diet
digest
disable
disease
disinfect
dispensary
dissect
doctor
dressing
drug
dumb
elixir
embryo
emergency
epidemic
ether
examination
examine
faint
fatal
feature
fever
figure
fit
fitness
forceps
fracture
function
gauze
germ
gland
head
heal

health
healthy
hear
hearing
heart
heartbeat
holistic
homeopathic
hospital
human
hydrotherapy
hygiene
hypo
hypocritic oath
ICU
ill
illness
immune
immunity
incision
incurable
infect
infectious
infirmity
injure
injury
inoculate
intern
internal
invalid
isolate
itch
joint
laboratory
lesion
life
ligament
limb

liniment
live
liver
lung
M.D.
malignant
manual
marrow
massage
medical
medicate
medication
medicine
medico
member
mental
microbe
microscope
mind
muscle
naturopath
needle
nerve
neurology
neurotic
nostrum
nurse
nutrition
observation
oculist
office
ointment
old
on-call
operate
operation
opiate
optic

optical
oral
organ
osteopath
pain
palate
panacea
paralyze
parasite
patient
peroxide
pharmacy
phobia
physical
physician
pill
plague
poison
practice
prescribe
prescription
prevent
prevention
psychiatric
pulse
pupil
quack
quarantine
quick
radium
reaction
recover
recuperate
reflex
relax
relief
relieve
remedy

research
resident
resistance
respiration
resuscitate
revive
rounds
run
salve
sanitary
sanitorium
sawbones
scalpel
scar
sedative
see
serum
shock
shot
shrink
sick
smell
smile
sneeze
sore
specialist
speech
spinal

spleen
splint
sports
squint
sterilize
stethoscope
stimulant
stomach
suffer
surgeon
surgery
susceptible
suture
sweat
symptom
tablet
taste
teeth
temperature
tendon
test
therapist
therapy
thermometer
tissue
tonic
tooth
touch

tourniquet
tranquilizer
transfusion
trauma
treat
treatment
triage
unconscious
vaccinate
vein
vertebra
victim
virus
vision
visual
vitamin
ward
weak
weakness
weight
well
well-being
wound
wrinkle
X-ray
young

Medical and Health Phrases

Fit as a fiddle . . . hang out a shingle . . . healthy, wealthy and wise . . . is there a doctor in the house? . . . intensive care unit . . . isolation ward . . . just what the doctor ordered . . . no pain, no gain . . . patent medicine . . . run a temperature . . . serious case . . . shake well before using . . . shot in the arm . . . take the cure . . . what to do until the doctor comes . . . wonder drug.

Entry Example

I like to buy at (store) because . . . they TREAT me square, their fresh food is a TONIC to my table, and I needn't DOCTOR my budget to keep it from feeling PAIN.

MILITARY

action	battle	cold war
adjutant	bayonet	colonel
advance	bazooka	combat
aggression	beat	command
aggressor	belligerent	commander
aim	blackout	commission
air force	blitz	company
alliance	blockade	conflict
allied forces	bomb	conquer
ally	bombard	conscript
ambush	boot camp	contraband
ammunition	border	corporal
annihilate	branch	corps
armament	brave	courage
armed forces	brig	court martial
armistice	brigade	cover
armor	bugle	decisive
armory	bullet	defeat
arms	cadet	defend
army	caisson	defensive
artillery	camouflage	defoliate
assault	camp	demolish
assembly	campaign	deploy
atom	cannon	desert
attache	canteen	destroy
attack	captain	detail
AWOL	carnage	devastate
ballistic	casualty	dig in
barrack	cavalry	disable
barrage	censor	disarm
barricade	chaplain	discharge
base	charge	division
basic training	clash	DMZ
battalion	club	doughboy

draft
dragoon
drill
drum
dugout
duration
duty
enemy
engage
engagement
enlist
entrench
expedition
field
fight
fire
firebomb
flag
flak
flank
flare
foe
force
formation
fort
fortify
fortress
four-star
foxhole
front
frontier
furlough
gallantry
garrison
gas
general
GI
goldbrick

grenade
guard
guardhouse
guerrilla
gun
gunner
gunnery
headquarters
helicopter
helmet
hero
heroic
hitch
honorable
    discharge
hostage
hostile
hostility
infantry
invade
invasion
invincible
juggernaut
kill
knight
KP
lance
latrine
leave
liberate
lieutenant
line
lose
loss
M-1
machine gun
major
maneuver

march
marine
marksman
marshal
martial
MASH
mass
menace
mess
MIA
militarist
military
militia
mine
missile
mission
mobilization
mobilize
mortar
munitions
napalm
national guard
navy
neutral
neutrality
nuclear war
objective
occupation
occupy
offense
offensive
officer
operation
opponent
oppose
order
orderly
ordnance

outbreak
outflank
overcome
pacifist
parade
parapet
paratroops
pass
patriot
patrol
peace
pillbox
pilot
pineapple
pistol
platoon
POW
power
prisoner
private
PT
quarters
raid
rampart
range
rank
rear
reconnaissance
reconnoiter
recruit
regiment
repel
rescue
reserve
resist
retreat

rifle
rocket
rookie
saber
salute
salvo
scout
security
sentry
sergeant
serve
service
shell
shield
shoot
shot
shrapnel
siege
slacker
slaughter
slay
sniper
soldier
spy
squad
squadron
staff
strafe
strategy
strife
strike
struggle
submachine
gun
submit
surrender

surround
survive
sword
tactics
tank
taps
target
tent
territory
train
treaty
trench
triumph
troops
ultimatum
uniform
VA
vanquish
veteran
victor
victorious
victory
volley
volunteer
war
warfare
warlord
warrior
weapon
win
wipe out
withdraw
wound
yield

Military Phrases

Act of war . . . agent orange . . . aide de camp . . . all quiet on the Western front . . . at ease . . . bug gun . . . bow and arrow . . . brass hat . . . brink of war . . . call to arms . . . charge of the light brigade . . . chief of staff . . . Civil War . . . commander in chief . . . conscientious objector . . . counter attack . . . declare war . . . demilitarized zone . . . don't shoot till you see the whites of their eyes . . . draft dodger . . . draft exempt . . . farewell to arms . . . fifth column . . . firing squad . . . force of arms . . . forward march . . . gas attack . . . gas mask . . . "git thar fustest with the mostest" . . . going great guns . . . hand to hand . . . knights of the round table . . . line of defense . . . martial law . . . meet one's Waterloo . . . military police . . . mine field . . . Minute Man . . . missing in action . . . no man's land . . . over the top . . . poison gas . . . prisoner of war . . . private first class . . . Purple Heart . . . rally round the flag . . . raw recruit . . . ready, aim, fire! . . . red badge of courage . . . Rough Rider . . . secret agent . . . shell shock . . . shoulder arms . . . state of siege . . . sue for peace . . . sure as shooting . . . surprise attack . . . survival of the fittest . . . take cover . . . the blue and the gray . . . they shall not pass . . . theirs but to do and die . . . tide of battle . . . Trojan Horse . . . unconditional surrender . . . valley of death . . . wage war . . . war and peace . . . war is hell . . . when knighthood was in flower . . . World War.

Entry Example

I like (laundry soap) because . . . I've declared a washday ARMISTICE since scoring a decided VICTORY over Monday's BATTLES with this modern WEAPON that DEFEATS dirt quickly, easily and safely.

MONEY AND WEALTH

bill
cash
centavo
centime
check
coin
confederate
counterfeit
credit
credit card
crown
currency
deutsche mark
dime
dollar
drachma
forgery
franc
gilder

gold coin
gold-digger
grasping
greed
greedy
greenback
half dollar
kite
krone
lay away
lean
lira
lucre
mark
mint
moola
negotiable
nickel
pence

penny
peso
plastic
pound
quarter
rich
ruble
securities
shekel
shilling
sovereign
sterling
treasury
treasury notes
wealthy
widow's mite
worth
yen
yuan

Money and Wealth Phrases

A day late and a dollar short . . . a penny for your thoughts . . . a penny saved is a penny earned . . . coin a phrase . . . check mate . . . fat cat . . . horn of plenty . . . lean 'n mean . . . make a mint . . . make both ends meet . . . Midas touch . . . money is the root of all evil . . . not worth a hill of beans . . . where the buck stops.

Money Madness

This man was having a great time at a party when he suddenly discovered his wallet was missing. He leaped up on a table and shouted to the crowd, "My wallet is missing. It's got over $400 in it. I'll give $50 to anyone who finds it and returns it."

A voice across the room yelled, "I'll give $100!"

Things are so bad in Texas, J. R. Ewing is now known as I. O. Ewing.

When the banker asked the man applying for a loan, "Could I have a statement?"

The loan seeker replied, "I'm optimistic."

There's more to life than money . . . and I've had quite enough of the other, thank you!

Broke is when you save your money for a rainy day—and you live in Seattle.

MUSIC

accent
accompani-
   ment
accompany
accordion
air
album
alto
amplifier
andante
aria
arrangement
bagpipe
band
bandstand
banjo
bar
baritone
baroque
bass
bassoon
baton
beat
bells
blues
bow
brass
bridge
bugle
canon
carol
castanet
CD
cello

chamber
chant
chimes
choir
chord
chorus
clarinet
classical
combo
compose
composer
concert
conduct
conductor
cornet
croon
cymbal
disc
discord
drum
duet
ensemble
etude
falsetto
fanfare
fiddle
fife
finale
flat
flute
forte
glockenspiel
gong
groovy

guitar
harmonica
harmonize
harmony
harp
harpsichord
hi-fi
high C
hit
horn
hum
hymn
improvise
instrument
jam
jazz
jitterbug
jive
kazoo
kettle
key
keyboard
keynote
lead
leader
lute
lyre
lyric
madrigal
major
mandolin
march
measure
medley

mellow	prelude	stereophonic
melody	prima donna	strings
minor	quartet	strum
minstrel	quintet	studio
movement	ragtime	suite
music	range	sweet
musical	recital	swing
musician	record	symphony
mute	reed	syncopate
natural	register	tempo
note	rest	tenor
oboe	rhapsody	theme
octave	rhythm	tone
off key	rock	traps
opera	rock 'n roll	trill
operetta	roll	trio
opus	sax	trombone
oratorio	saxophone	trumpet
orchestra	scale	tuba
organ	score	tune up
overture	send	tune
passage	serenade	tweeter
pedal	sharp	ukulele
percussion	sheet music	upbeat
phonograph	sing	valve
phrase	solo	viola
piano	sonata	violin
piccolo	song	voice
piece	soprano	volume
pipe	sound	whistle
pitch	speaker	wind
plain song	spinet	woofer
platter	staccato	xylophone
play	staff	yodel
pluck	stand	zither

Music Phrases

And the night shall be filled with music . . . baby grand . . . beat the band . . . call the tune . . . carry a tune . . . face the music . . . hit a high note . . . hit parade . . . in the groove . . . jam session . . . lead the band . . . lost chord . . . music goes round and round . . . music hath charms to soothe the savage beast . . . music to the ear . . . out of tune . . . pipes of Pan . . . play by ear . . . sax appeal . . . say it with music . . . song is over, but the melody lingers on . . . strike the right note . . . Tin Pan Alley . . . toot your own horn . . . unfinished symphony.

Jingle Example

If HARMONY is what you crave,
Go get a TUBA Burma-Shave!

Entry Example

I buy (juice) because . . . NATURAL flavor brings MAJOR satisfaction for a MEDLEY of nourishment in the KEY of "C," providing energizing refreshment in nothing FLAT.

MYTH AND LEGEND

Adonis	goddess	oracle
Agamemnon	golden fleece	Paris
Antigone	griffin	Pegasus
Aphrodite	Guenevere	Persephone
Arabian nights	Hades	Pleiades
Arthur	Helen	Poseidon
Atlas	Hercules	Psyche
Cupid	Holy Grail	round table
dragon	Jason	Scheherazade
dryad	Jove	siren
elf	Jupiter	sorcerer
epic	knight	Styx
Eros	Mars	trial
fairy	Medusa	troll
fairy queen	mermaid	underworld
faun	mortal	unicorn
flood	naiad	Venus
giant	Neptune	werewolf
goblin	nymph	wizard
god	Odysseus	Zeus

Myth and Legend Phrases

As strong as Hercules . . . epic movie . . . flying sorcerer . . . go to hades . . . he's a real Adonis . . . nymphomania . . . Poseidon affair . . . wizard of ahs.

Quotation

"We will not find scientific or historical truth in mythology. But we will find poetic truth. And poetic truth may be all the truth that men will ever know."
Bergen Evans

NATIONAL

Afghanistan	Republic	Gambia
Africa	Chad	geography
African	Chile	Ghana
Albania	China	Gibraltar
Algeria	Chinese	global
alien	citizen	globe
America	colony	Greece
American	commonwealth	Guinea
Anglo-Saxon	Congo	Guinea Bissau
Angola	country	gypsy
Ankara	Cuba	Hawaii
Arabic	Cypress	Hindu
Asia	Czech	Holland
Asiatic	Czechoslovakia	Hong Kong
Australia	Dahomey	Hungary
Austria	Denmark	Iceland
Bahamas	Dijibouti	independence
Belgium	district	independent
Bhutan	dominion	India
Bohemia	Dutch	Indonesia
Botswana	East Germany	Iran
Brazil	Egypt	Iraq
Britain	empire	Ireland
British	England	Israel
Brunei	English	Italy
Bulgaria	Eskimo	Ivory Coast
Burkina Faso	Ethiopia	Jamaica
Burma	Europe	Jammu
Burundi	federal	Japan
Cambodia	Finland	Java
Cameroon	foreign	Jordan
Canada	Formosa	Kashmir
Central	France	Kenya
African	Gabon	kingdom

Korea	Nigeria	Somali
kosher	Norway	South Africa
language	Nubia	sovereign
Laos	occidental	Soviet
Latin	oriental	Spain
Lebanon	Pakistan	Sri Lanka
Lesotho	Panama	state
Libya	Papua- New	Sudan
Liechtenstein	Guinea	Swaziland
Luxembourg	People's	Sweden
Malawi	Republic of	Switzerland
Malaysia	China	Syria
Mali	Peru	Tanzania
Masao	Philippines	Thailand
Mauritania	Poland	Tibet
Mauritius	Portugal	Togo
Mexico	province	Tunisia
Monaco	region	Turkey
monarchy	republic	universal
Mongolia	Roman	USSR
Morocco	Romania	Vietnam
Mozambique	Russia	Wales
Namibia	Rwanda	West Germany
nation	Samoa	world
national	Sardinia	Yank
native	Scotland	Yugoslavia
Nepal	SenegalSicily	Zambia
Netherlands	Sierra Leone	Zimbabwe
New Zealand	Sikkim	
Niger	Singapore	

National Phrases

Abie's Irish Rose . . . all Greek to me . . . all the tea
in China . . . American way of life . . . Britannia rules
the waves . . . canny Scot . . . castles in Spain . . . Chile
reception . . . chosen people . . . Danish pastry . . . down

Mexico way . . . Dutch treat . . . Dutch uncle . . . East is East and West is West . . . Emerald Isle . . . fifty million Frenchmen can't be wrong . . . fine Italian hand . . . French dressing . . . frugal as a Scot . . . get in Dutch . . . go Dutch . . . go native . . . Hungarian goulash . . . Irish stew . . . melancholy Dane . . . never the twain shall meet . . . Omar, the tent maker . . . Russian dressing . . . Siamese twins . . . so near and yet so foreign . . . something rotten in Denmark . . . South American way . . . strong as Gibraltar . . . sun never sets on the British Empire . . . there'll always be an England . . . Turkish delight . . . Uncle Sam . . . vive la France . . . wearing of the green . . . when in Rome, do as the Romans do.

Entry Example

I shop at (department store) because . . . their suits feature SCOTCH thriftiness, FRENCH verve, ENGLISH excellence, AMERICAN style and UNIVERSAL appeal!

NAVAL

admiral
aft
aircraft
  carrier
anchor
anchorage
ashore
bail
battleship
beach
becalm
blockade
boat
bombard
bosun
bow
bridge
brig
broadside
buccaneer
cabin
calm
cannonade
capsize
captain
cargo
carrier
cast off
castaway
channel
clipper
coast
coast guard
commander

commodore
compass
convoy
craft
crew
cruise
cruiser
current
deck
destroyer
dock
dreadnought
drift
drydock
engage
engineer
ensign
fathom
fireman
first mate
flagship
flattop
fleet
float
flotilla
fore
forward
founder
freighter
frigate
funnel
gangplank
gangway
gear

gob
grapple
gunboat
gunwale
harbor
hardtack
hatch
heave to
helm
hold
hull
ironclad
keel
keelhaul
ketch
knot
landfall
landlubber
launch
league
lieutenant
life preserver
lifebelt
lifeboat
line
liner
log
lookout
main deck
mainmast
man o'war
marine
mariner
maroon

mast
mate
merchant
  marine
mine
minesweeper
moor
nautical
naval
navigate
navy
oar
ocean
officer
offshore
overboard
patrol
petty officer
pier
pilot
piracy
pirate
poop
port
porthole
prow
PT boat
raft
rail
ram
rear admiral

rigging
row
sail
sailor
salvage
salvo
schooner
scurvy
scuttle
scuttlebutt
sea
Seabee
seaman
seaplane
seapower
seasick
shell
ship
shipmate
shipshape
shore leave
shore patrol
skipper
sloop
smokestack
SOS
spar
squadron
starboard
steer
stern

steward
stoker
stowaway
strand
submarine
submerge
superstructure
supply
surface
swashbuckler
swell
tanker
tar
tide
tiller
tonnage
torpedo
tow
transport
turret
U-boat
underway
vessel
voyage
wake
warship
watch
wave
wharf
yaw

Naval Phrases

Abandon ship . . . able seaman . . . all at sea . . . all hands on deck . . . any port in a storm . . . Barnacle Bill . . . boarding party . . . bon voyage . . . cast adrift . . .

crow's nest . . . depth charge . . . don't give up the ship
. . . down the ways . . . down to the sea in ships . . .
flotsam and jetsam . . . freedom of the seas . . . full
speed ahead . . . go to the bottom . . . high seas . . . life
saver . . . Mae West . . . maiden voyage . . . make port
. . . man overboard . . . Mutiny on the Bounty . . .
mutiny on the high seas . . . naval base . . . naval maneuvers . . . Old Ironsides . . . old salt . . . open boat . . .
over the side . . . Popeye the Sailor . . . pull away . . .
rough sea . . . run aground . . . sail the seven seas . . .
sea battle . . . sea rations . . . ships that pass in the night
. . . sighted sub, sank same . . . smoke screen . . . smooth
sailing . . . storm at sea . . . strike her colors . . . sunk
without trace . . . sunken ship . . . task force . . . 20,000
Leagues Under the Sea . . . Two Years Before the Mast
. . . under forced draft . . . under full sail . . . walk the
plank . . . women and children first.

Entry Example

I use (cold medicine) because . . . it helps break the
cold BLOCKAGE, gives me FREEDOM FROM THE
SNEEZE, and lets me win a BIG NASAL VICTORY!

NUCLEAR

A-bomb
activate
age
armament
arms
atom
atom bomb
atomic
blast
bombard
capability
carbon
cell
charge
cloud
cobalt
combustion
compound
condenser
control
conversion
convert
cosmic
cyclotron
destroy
destruction
detonate
device
disarmament
discharge
disintegrate
electron
element
energy

engineering
experiment
explode
explosive
fallout
fire
fission
flash
force
fuel
fuse
fusion
future
generator
H-bomb
harness
heat
helium
hydrogen
ion
magnetic
mass
matter
medicine
megaton
melt down
missile
molecule
mushroom
negative
neutralize
neutron
nuclear
nucleus

particle
peace
physics
piles
plutonium
polarization
policy
positive
potential
power
pressure
proliferation
proton
pulverize
radiate
radiation
radioactive
radium
raid
ray
reaction
reactor
release
research
safety
science
scientific
shatter
shelter
shield
source
split
static
stockpile

structure	transmute	vaporize
survival	trigger	war
theory	tube	waste
trace	ultraviolet	wave
transfer	uranium	weapon
transformation	vapor	X-ray

Nuclear Phrases

Atomic Age . . . atomic energy . . . atomic pile . . . chain reaction . . . conservation of energy . . . critical mass . . . Geiger counter . . . ground zero . . . heavy water . . . Manhattan Project . . . mushroom cloud . . . New Era . . . power plant . . . push-button war . . . shock wave . . . splitting the atom . . . spontaneous combustion . . . top secret . . . total war . . . up and atom!

Entry Example

I like (oatmeal) because . . . it's the NUCLEUS of a solid breakfast, with food ELEMENTS skillfully COMPOUNDED for maximum ENERGY. A POWERFUL WEAPON against undernourishment.

PATRIOTIC

allegiance
America
American
arms
army
banner
battle
bold
brave
bravery
bugle
capitol
cause
challenge
cheer
chivalry
citizen
colors
command
conquer
constitution
corps
country
courage
dare
daring
dauntless
defend
democracy
devoting
drum
duty
eagle
emblem

enlist
ensign
equal
equality
fanfare
fatherland
fight
flag
forbearers
forefathers
fortitude
forward
free
freedom
gallant
gallantry
glory
guard
heritage
hero
heroic
heroine
heroism
history
honor
independence
independent
justice
land
law
leader
legion
liberty
loyal

loyalty
march
marine
medal
mettle
monument
motherland
muster
nation
national
native
navy
parade
patriot
patriotic
patriotism
pioneer
pledge
power
powerful
prepare
pride
protect
prowess
rally
rebel
republic
reserve
respect
revolt
revolution
rights
sacrifice
sailor

salute	struggle	uphold
sentry	summon	valiant
serve	symbol	valor
soldier	tradition	veteran
sovereign	traitor	victory
spirit	triumph	volley
stand	U.S.A.	volunteer
standard	unfurl	vote
stars	uniform	war
state	union	wave
stripes	union jack	Yank
strong	unite	Yankee

Patriotic Phrases

American way of life . . . be prepared . . . big stick . . . Boston Tea Party . . . call to arms . . . conceived in liberty . . . Declaration of Independence . . . do your bit . . . don't give up the ship . . . father of his country . . . fife and drum . . . founding fathers . . . four freedoms . . . Fourth of July . . . free and equal . . . freedom of speech . . . gem of the ocean . . . give me liberty or give me death . . . hats off, our flag is passing by . . . home of the brave . . . I regret that I have but one life to give for my country . . . in union there is strength . . . Independence Day . . . land of the Free . . . law and order . . . let freedom ring . . . liberty bell . . . love it or leave it . . . make the world safe for democracy . . . medal of honor . . . Memorial Day . . . Minute Man . . . Monroe Doctrine . . . my country, right or wrong . . . National Guard . . . no taxation without representation . . . of thee I sing . . . Old Glory . . . Old Ironpower and the glory . . . rally 'round the flag boys . . . ramparts we watch . . . red, white and blue . . . remember the Alamo . . . remember the Maine . . . rough riders . . . Spirit of '76 . . . Star Spangled Banner . . . Stars and Stripes Forever . . . Statue of Liberty . . . the Blue and the Gray

. . . Uncle Sam . . . united we stand, divided we fall . .
. we the people . . . Yankee Doodle . . . Yanks are
coming.

Entry Example

An urchin once got on the sly
Explosives for FOURTH OF JULY.
But his father found out
What the kid was about.
He saw RED, then turned WHITE, and BLEW high!

PHOTOGRAPHY

action
album
aperture
automatic
background
blackout
blow-up
blur
bulb
cables
camcorder
camera
candid
catch
cinema-
  tography
clear
click
close-up
color
commercial
composition
contact
contrast
crop
darkroom
depict
depth
detail
develop
distance
distort
distortion
double

exposure
dupe
duplicate
enlarge
enlargement
etch
exhibit
exhibition
expose
exposure
fade
field
film
filter
finish
flash
floodlight
focal
focus
frame
glossy
graphic
halftone
hazy
high speed
highlight
hue
illustrate
image
Kodak
lens
light
matt
miniature

model
montage
mount
movie
mug
negative
night
original
overexposure
panorama
paste-up
perspective
photo
photograph
photographer
picture
pix
plate
portrait
portray
pose
positive
print
projection
projector
proofrange
red eye
reduce
reel
reflect
register
reproduce
retake
retouch

roll	silhouette	supplies
scene	sleeves	tint
scenic	slide	tintype
screen	snap	tone
separation	snapshot	touch up
shade	special effects	transparency
shadow	spectacle	tripod
sharp	speed	video
shoot	spotlight	view
shot	still	vision
shutter	studio	vista
shutterbug	subject	vivid

Photographic Phrases

Action shot . . . black and white . . . camera never lies . . . credit line . . . double exposure . . . family portrait . . . field of vision . . . figure study . . . graphic art . . . hold it! . . . it's a snap! . . . lights, camera, action! . . . long shot . . . out of focus . . . out of range . . . photo finish . . . range finder . . . rogues' gallery . . . say cheese . . . stop action . . . time exposure . . . watch the birdie . . . wide range.

Entry Example

I like (ketchup) because . . . its POSITIVE flavor helps DEVELOP appetite and turns an ordinary PLATE into a delightful dish that HIGHLIGHTS any meal.

POLITICS AND GOVERNMENT

absentee ballot
acclamation
accountability
act
address
adjourn
administration
aide
also-ran
amendment
anarchy
appeal
assassin
assembly
aye
backer
ballot
bandwagon
bill
Bill of Rights
bloc
bolt
booth
boss
branch
bylaws
cabinet
campaign
candidate
canvass
capital
Capitol
carry
caucus

chairman
chamber
closure
club
college
committee
Communist
conclave
conference
Congress
conservative
constituent
constitution
contender
control
convention
dark horse
deadlock
debate
defeat
delegate
democracy
Democrat
democratic
diplomat
donkey
draft
elect
election
electioneer
electoral
    elephant
endorse
enroll

filibuster
first lady
floor
GOP
gerrymander
govern
government
governor
gravel
hearing
House
impeach
incumbent
Independent
issue
judicial
junket
justice
keynote
labor
landslide
law
laws
leader
legislate
legislation
legislator
legislature
liberal
Libertarian
lobby
lobbyist
logrolling
lose

machine
majority
mayor
meeting
minority
monarchy
motion
move
mugwump
name
nay
nominate
office
officer
official
opponent
opposition
Parliament
partisan
party
pass
patronage
petition
pigeonhole
plank
platform
pledge
plurality
policy
political
politician
politics

poll
popular
precinct
preside
president
primary
prime minister
pro tem
procedure
Progressive
public
quorum
radical
rally
recess
red
register
represent
representative
republic
Republican
resolution
results
rider
rival
roll call
rule
run
secretary
Senate
Senator
seniority

serve
session
sheriff
slate
Socialist
speaker
speaker of the
  house
speech
stand
statesman
statesperson
successor
support
Supreme Court
tabled
term
theocracy
ticket
treasurer
unanimous
union
veto
vice president
victory
volunteer
vote
ward
Washington
Whig
White House
win

Political and Governmental Phrases

Advise and consent . . . balance the budget . . . by popular demand . . . campaign promise . . . cast a ballot

. . . chairman of the board . . . claim victory . . . concede . . . dark horse . . . delegate at large . . . domestic issue . . . favorite son or daughter . . . foreign affairs . . . foreign policy . . . foreign relations . . . front runner . . . gag rule . . . get out the vote . . . Grand Old Party . . . grass roots . . . hat in the ring . . . higher wages, shorter hours . . . House of Representatives . . . I do not choose to run . . . lame duck . . . law of the land . . . left wing . . . loyal opposition . . . make a motion . . . monster rally . . . New Deal . . . New Frontier . . . Old guard . . . on the calendar . . . out of office . . . parliamentary law . . . party line . . . party member . . . pressure group . . . rank and file . . . ride his coattails . . . rig an election . . . right wing . . . rules of order . . . run for office . . . running mate . . . secret ballot . . . slush fund . . . smoke-filled room . . . soapbox orator . . . special session . . . split ticket . . . State of the Union . . . steam roller . . . steering committee . . . straight ticket . . . straw vote . . . stuff the ballot box . . . take me to your leader . . . take the floor . . . take the lead . . . take the stump . . . the ayes have it . . . the first lady . . . the old order changeth . . . the people's choice . . . two-party system . . . voting booth . . . wide majority . . . win in the walk . . . yield the floor . . . you can't fight City Hall.

Entry Example

I serve my guests (soda pop) because . . . it's my CANDIDATE for the FAVORITE American drink, its PLATFORM is delicious flavor plus economy, and it WINS VOTES at all PARTIES.

Illustration

(Excerpt from my forthcoming book, *Recipes of the Rich & Famous*) I cast my BALLOT for every recipe in this book because each is a CANDIDATE for winning VOTES at dinners, luncheons, and the like. I make a MOTION that each be tried, from time to time, in one's own kitchen. Only then will we perhaps be able to single out the favorites because all are excellent and taste-worthy. They're certain to be the PEOPLE'S CHOICE, by a wide MAJORITY, at all PARTIES. Enjoy!

Political Prank

Recently a white rhinoceros was donated to the zoo in (city). That completes the cities collection of albinos when you consider the white elephant who resides on capital hill.

POSTAL

address
addressee
affix
airmail
arrive
bag
box
bulk mail
bundle
C.O.D.
cancel
cancellation
card
carrier
carrier
carry
carton
certify
claim
class
clerk
collect
convey
correspond
correspond-
  ence
courier
cover
deliver
delivery
deposit
destination
dispatch
domestic

enclose
enclosure
envelope
express
fast
fee
flap
foreign
form
forward
fragile
freight
general
  delivery
glue
ground
gum
handle
incoming
indemnity
indicia
insure
label
letter
lick
line
local
lock box
mail
mail carrier
mailbox
message
meter
missive

notification
notify
occupant
open
outgoing
P.O.
pack
package
parcel
parcel post
philatelist
philately
pick up
pony express
post
post office box
post office
postage
postal
postcard
postman
postmark
postmaster
postpaid
prepaid
priority
R.F.D.
rate
receipt
receive
register
return
route
rush

sack	special	truck
scale	speed	unsealed
scrawl	stamp	via
seal	station	weigh
send	stick	whistle
sender	surface	wrap
ship	tie	wrapper
shipment	trace	write
sign	transit	zip code
signature	transmit	zone
slot	transport	

Postal Phrases

Address unknown . . . Book Rate . . . cash on delivery . . . dead letter office . . . direct mail . . . drop a line . . . Express mail . . . first class . . . fourth class . . . handle with care . . . having wonderful time, wish you were here . . . junk mail . . . lost in transit . . . mail early for Christmas . . . mail order . . . mailing list . . . neither snow, nor rain, nor dark of night shall stay these couriers from the swift completion of their appointed rounds . . . opened by mistake . . . overseas mail . . . playing post office . . . postage due . . . postal inspector . . . return to sender . . . rural free delivery . . . rural route . . . second class . . . special delivery . . . special handling . . . stamp collector . . . the mail must go through . . . the postman always rings twice . . . third class . . . this package may be opened for postal inspection . . . to whom it may concern . . . undeliverable as addressed.

Entry Example

(Freight shipping company) carefully PACKAGES your merchandise for EXPRESS DELIVERY. We

HANDLE IT WITH CARE all along the ROUTE, always standing behind our CLAIM of excellence.

PRINTING AND PUBLISHING

accept
agent
alphabet
antiquarian
art
artist
artwork
author
bind
binding
bleed
bluelines
boards
book
booklet
border
bound
bulk
camera-ready
capital
card
case bound
catalog
chapbook
chapter
circular
classified
color
column
comma
complimentary

compose
composition
contract
copy
copyright
correct
cover
dash
deadline
delete
desktop
discounts
display
dot
draft
edit
edition
editor
elite
endpaper
engrave
errata
error
etch
extra
feature
final
flush
folio
font
foreword

form
four-color
front matter
galley
glossary
grammar
gripper
halftone
head
heading
hyphen
illustrations
imposition
impression
imprint
indent
initial
ink
insert
insertion
introduction
issue
jobber
journal
justify
label
layout
leading
leaflet
legible
letter

line
linotype
literary
literature
lock up
logo
magazine
make-up
manual
manuscript
margin
misprint
mock-up
newsletter
newspaper
notice
offset
page
pamphlet
paper
paperback
paragraph
PC
period
periodical
pica
plate
poem
poetic

poster
press
print
printer
promote
promotion
proof
proofread
proportional
publication
publish
punctuate
quotation
quote
read
recto
reduce
register
reject
release
relief
report
reporter
reproduce
reproduction
revise
royalty
rule
run

self-publishing
serial
sheet
shipping
signature
slug
space
spell
spelling
stationery
stock
story
style
subsidiary
subsidy
text
title
trade
trim
type
typeface
typesetting
typewrite
typist
vanity
verso
volume
write

Printing and Publishing Phrases

All the news that's fit to print . . . best seller . . . blue pencil . . . bold face . . . bound to please . . . dust cover . . . first draft . . . first edition . . . five-star final . . . form letter . . . hard cover . . . limited edition . . . lower case . . . on the press . . . printed matter . . . rare edition . .

. to be continued . . . truth is stranger than fiction . . .
upper case . . . you can't judge a book by its cover.

Entry Example

I like (ketchup) because . . . its INTRODUCTION
to any PLATE provides a VOLUME of eating enjoy-
ment that gives every meal a HAPPY ENDING.

RADIO AND TV

AC/DC
act
advertising
aerial
AM
amplify
announce
announcer
antenna
applause
audible
audience
audio
audition
back haul
band
battery
beam
broadcast
bulletin
cable
cables
camera
channel
circuit
close-up
color
commercial
communicate
communication
coverage
current
descrambler
dialogue

director
disc jockey
downlink
earphones
electronic
entertain
fade
flashback
FM
footage
frequency
gigihertz
ham
hear
hi-fi
hookup
horizontal
host
image
interference
K band
kilocycle
kilohertz
license
listen
live
loudspeaker
MC
megacycle
megahertz
microphone
mike
music
network

newscast
panel
performer
play
plug in
portable
preview
producer
production
program
propaganda
Q band
quiz
radio
rating
receive
reception
recording
rehearse
remote
remote control
repeat
review
satellite
scan
scramble
screen
script
see
send
set
shoot
show
sight

signal	tape	up link
SOS	telecast	VCR
sound	televise	vertical
soundtrack	television	video
speaker	transistor	videotape
spectacular	transmit	view
sponsor	tube	voice
spot	tune in	volume
static	tune out	watch
station	turn off	wavelength
stereo	turn on	writer
studio	TV	
survey	two-way	

Radio and TV Phrases

Air waves . . . before the mike . . . black and white
. . . call letters . . . clear channel . . . coast-to-coast
hookup . . . come in loud and clear . . . control room .
. . fade out . . . high fidelity . . . high frequency . . . late,
late show . . . living color . . . low frequency . . . master
of ceremonies . . . natural color . . . on the air . . . on
the beam . . . pay TV . . . picture tube . . . please stand
by . . . remote control . . . satellite dish . . . short wave
. . . sign off . . . soap opera . . . sound effects . . . special
announcement . . . special event . . . special report . . .
spot announcement . . . spin a record . . . station break
. . . studio audience . . . sustaining program . . . the next
voice you'll hear . . . TV dinner . . . TV or Not TV . .
. we interrupt this program . . . we pause for station
identification.

Entry Example

(Ketchup) is best because . . . SPONSORED by a
famous maker, its PROGRAM is to please the widest

AUDIENCE with richness that never FADES and flavor that's always ON THE BEAM.

RAILROAD

air brake
AmTrak
arrival
arrive
baggage
baggage car
berth
boiler
boxcar
brake
brakeman
cab
caboose
cannonball
car
carload
carry
cattle car
choo-choo
coach
coal
coal car
cog
collide
collision
commute
commuter
conductor
couple
cowcatcher
crew

crossing
crossroad
depart
departure
depot
derail
diesel
dining car
dispatch
dispatcher
drive
engine
engineer
express
fare
fireman
flatcar
flyer
freight
friction
fuel
gear
gondola
grade
handcar
haul
headlight
highball
horsepower
journey
junction

leave
limited
line
local
locomotive
monorail
motor
motorman
narrow-gauge
oil
passage
passenger
platform
power
puff
pull
pull in
Pullman
punch
rail
railroad
railway
rapid
ride
rider
roadbed
roundhouse
route
schedule
seat
shed

siding	subway	transport
signal	switch	transportation
sleeper	tender	travel
smoke	terminal	traveler
smokestack	throttle	trestle
special	ticket	trip
speed	tie	tunnel
spike	timetable	underground
station	token	washout
steam	track	wheel
steel	traction	whistle
stoke	train	yard
stop	tram	
streamliner	transit	

Railroad Phrases

All aboard . . . bar car . . . Casey Jones . . . catch a train . . . circus train . . . delayed en route . . . full speed ahead . . . grade crossing . . . Grand Central Station . . . Great Train Robbery . . . head-on collision . . . Iron Horse . . . little red caboose . . . long haul . . . lower berth . . . model railroad . . . observation car . . . on the right track . . . on the wrong track . . . Orient Express . . . rapid transit . . . ride the rails . . . right of way . . . rolling stock . . . sharp curve ahead . . . signal tower . . . sleeping car . . . station master . . . steam engine . . . tell him where to get off . . . ticket agent . . . ticket office . . . ties that bind . . . Union Pacific . . . upper berth . . . whistle stop . . . working on the railroad.

Entry Example

I shop at (store) because . . . TRAINED to appreciate quality and thrift, I'll RIDE along with their LINE of top GRADE products and prices others can't TIE.

RELIGION

altar
apostle
baptism
bar mitzvah
belief
believer
Bible
Bible school
bishop
books
burial ground
Calvary
catechism
cathedral
Catholic
chalice
chapel
charity
choir
Christ
Christian
church
clergy
cloister
commandments
communion
confession
confirmation
congregation
consecrate
conservative
convent
creed
cross

crucifix
disciple
doctrine
dogma
epistle
evangelical
faith
fasting
father
fellowship
flagellant
God
good news
gospel
grace
Grail
great spirit
healer
heaven
Hebrew school
hell
holy
Holy Ghost
Holy Land
holy writ
hymn
Jerusalem
Jesus
Jewish
kingdom
Koran
lama
lamasery
Lazarus

Lutheran
Magdalene
meditation
Messiah
metaphysical
Methodist
minister
ministry
miracle
monk
Moslem
mother
narthex
nave
non-denomi-
  national
nun
ordain
ordination
orthodox
parable
parish
pastor
path
penitent
Pentecost
pew
pilgrim
pilgrimage
pope
prayer
preacher
priest
prophet

Protestant	saint	testament
psalm	sanctuary	testimony
pulpit	savior	theology
purgatory	scripture	tithe
rabbi	seder	tongues
reader	seminary	torah
redemption	sermon	translation
reformed	sin	vacation
reign	soul	veda
retreat	spirit	vespers
revival	sun dancer	vestiary
rocky road	Sunday school	vestments
rosary	synagogue	vestry
sacraments	tabernacle	way
sacred	temple	word
sacristy	temptation	worship

Religious Phrases

By the grace of God . . . chapter and verse . . . crown of thorns . . . faith can move mountains . . . heaven sent . . . King James Version . . . loaves and fishes . . . pray without ceasing . . . say a prayer for me . . . Sermon on the Mount . . . stages of the Cross . . . straight and narrow.

Slogan

Let FAITH REIGN in your life for a radiant SPIRIT.

Religious Repartee

"I'm not saying she's a bad cook," said the young man about his future mother-in-law, "but I know now why her family prays before every meal."

ROYALTY

abdicate
aristocracy
aristocrat
baron
bow
castle
cavalier
chieftain
coronation
coronet
count
countess
court
courtier
crest
crown
curtsy
czar
czarina
domain
dominion
duchess
duchy
duke
dynasty
earl
emperor
empire
empress
figurehead

heir
herald
imperial
kaiser
king
kingdom
kneel
knight
knighted
knighthood
knightly
lady
lord
lordship
maharajah
maharani
majestic
majesty
marquis
mikado
milady
monarch
monarchy
nabob
nobility
noble
palace
patrician
peer
peerage

plume
potentate
prince
princely
princess
privileged
queen
queenly
rajah
rank
realm
regal
reign
royal
royalty
rule
ruler
scepter
shah
sir
sire
sovereign
subject
sultan
sword
throne
title
viceroy
viscount

Royalty Phrases

Absolute monarchy . . . all the king's horses and all the king's men . . . ascend the throne . . . blue blood . . . coat of arms . . . court jester . . . crown jewels . . . crown prince . . . divine right . . . every inch a king . . . fit for a king . . . heir apparent . . . heir to the throne . . . his or her majesty . . . his or her royal highness . . . House of Lords . . . knight errant . . . lady-in-waiting . . . long live the King . . . monarch of all I survey . . . off with his head! . . . palace guard . . . pomp and ceremony . . . power behind the throne . . . Queen of Hearts . . . red carpet . . . round table . . . royal blood . . . royal family . . . royal purple . . . the King and I . . . the king can do no wrong . . . to the manor born . . . to the queen's taste . . . uneasy lies the head that wears a crown . . . when knighthood was in flower.

Entry Example

I serve my guest this famous drink because . . . NOBLE in heritage, PRINCELY in flavor, and worth a KING'S ransom, it REIGNS supreme in the DOMAIN of refreshment.

SAFETY

accident	escape ramp	obey
accidental	emergency	observe
acid	fall	padlock
aid	first aid	pain
alarm	fix	peril
alert	foolproof	poison
armor	go	police
assist	goggles	precaution
avoid	guard	prepare
bandage	guardian	prevent
beware	harm	prevention
bolt	hazard	protect
bother	heed	protection
brake	heedless	railing
care	helmet	reckless
carefree	help	regret
careful	horn	remorse
careless	hurt	repair
caustic	ignore	rescue
caution	injure	resuscitate
cautious	injury	revive
chance	inoculate	risk
check up	insurance	rule
child-proof	key	safe
collide	life	safeguard
collision	lifeguard	safekeeping
crash	lifesaver	safeness
crossing	lock	safety
danger	lookout	save
dare	medicine	secure
daring	menace	security
doctor	mishap	shield
drop	neglect	sign
drown	notice	signal

slip	traffic	warn
sorry	trip	warning
stop	trouble	wary
stumble	vaccinate	watch
survive	vault	wreck
threat	vigilant	

Safety Phrases

Alert today, alive tomorrow . . . an ounce of prevention is worth a pound of cure . . . artificial respiration . . . be prepared . . . cause and effect . . . common sense . . . cross at the green, not in between . . . daring young man on the flying trapeze . . . didn't know it was loaded . . . don't be half safe . . . look both ways . . . fire extinguisher . . . forewarned is forearmed . . . guardian angel . . . handle with care . . . keep your eyes peeled . . . learn a lesson . . . look before you leap . . . mind your business . . . no smoking . . . on your toes . . . open carefully . . . pay attention . . . play it safe . . . proceed with caution . . . right of way . . . safe and sound . . . safety first . . . safety valve . . . safety zone . . . save your skin . . . sharp curve ahead . . . sink or swim . . . stop, look and listen . . . the life you save may be your won . . . under lock and key . . . watch where you're going . . . watch your step.

Entry Example

I like (frozen foods) because . . . they're my FIRST AID for quick meals, SAVING me extra TROUBLE in preparation when guests FALL in with WARNINGS.

SIZES AND SHAPES

acre	dense	height
amount	density	hexagon
angle	depth	high
area	diameter	huge
balance	diamond	inch
big	dimension	increase
body	diminish	king-size
border	diminutive	large
bound	dram	latitude
boundary	dwarf	league
box	empty	length
breadth	enormous	less
broad	expand	life-size
bulk	expanse	light
bushel	extent	Lilliputian
caliber	fat	little
capacity	fathom	long
carat	foot	longitude
circle	fraction	magnify
circular	full	mammoth
circumference	furlong	margin
close	gallon	mass
colossal	giant	matter
cone	gigantic	maxi
contract	gill	maximum
contraction	girth	measure
cube	grain	measurement
cubic	gram	medium
curvaceous	great	meter
curve	gross	metric system
cylinder	grow	micro
decrease	growth	midget
deep	half	mile
degree	heavy	mini

miniature	quantity	solid
minute	quart	space
more	quarter	sphere
narrow	range	square
oblong	ream	stunted
octagon	rectangle	tall
ounce	reduce	thick
oval	rod	thin
oversize	rotund	tiny
overweight	round	ton
parallel	ruler	tower
part	runt	trapezoid
pear	scale	triangle
peck	section	vast
pentagon	segment	volume
piece	shape	wafer thin
pint	short	wedge
portion	shrimp	weight
pound	shrink	whole
proportion	sizable	wide
pygmy	size	width
pyramid	small	yard

Size and Shape Phrases

A miss is as good as a mile . . . an ounce of prevention is worth a pound of cure . . . big as life and twice as natural . . . cut down to size . . . David and Goliath . . . eternal triangle . . . feel boxed in . . . girth of a nation . . . high, wide, and handsome . . . large economy size . . . larger than life . . . look far and wide . . . Mutt and Jeff . . . pyramid your profits . . . round and around . . . sell short . . . seven league boots . . . that's about the size of it . . . the bigger they are, the harder they fall . . . the long and short of it . . . through thick and thin . . . tip the scales . . . Tom Thumb . . . try this on for size . . . whole is the sum of its parts.

Entry Example

I'll visit the World's Fair again because . . . it's HIGH in educational value, WIDE in variety of sights to enjoy, and handsome in its VAST panorama— pleasing BIG and LITTLE visitors!

Size Smiles

Two PINTS make one cavort.

"Smiles" is the LONGEST word in the language—with a MILE between its first and last letters.

SPACE

A-Okay
accelerate
air
alien
aloft
altitude
ascend
asteroid
astral
astronaut
astronomer
astronomy
atmosphere
atomic
beam
blast off
booster
capsule
catapult
celestial
circle
comet
communicate
computer
constellation
control
cosmic
cosmos
countdown
course
density
descend
earth
earthling

eclipse
energy
explore
extra
  terrestrial
fission
flash
flight
float
fly
free fall
fuel
galaxy
globe
gravity
ground
heaven
height
high
hurl
hurtle
interplanetary
journey
Jupiter
land
landing
launch
lift-off
lunar
manned
Mars
Mercury
meteor
Milky Way

missile
momentum
monitor
moon
NASA
nebula
Neptune
nova
nuclear
observatory
orbit
pad
pilot
planet
planetary
plunge
Pluto
power
probe
projectile
propel
radar
range
revolve
rise
rocket
rotate
satellite
Saturn
send up
shoot
shot
shuttle
sky

skyward	stellar	upward
soar	summit	Uranus
solar	sun	vacuum
space suit	supernova	velocity
space	surface	Venus
spaceship	take off	voyage
speed	telescope	weightless
sphere	thrust	whirl
spin	track	world
sputnik	universe	zenith
star	unmanned	zoom
station	update	

Space Phrases

All systems are go . . . Cape Kennedy . . . center of gravity . . . craters of the moon . . . down to earth . . . escape velocity . . . flying saucer . . . get off the ground . . . guided missile . . . heavenly body . . . intelligent life . . . launching pad . . . light year . . . out of this world . . . outer space . . . panic button . . . point of no return . . . pressure suit . . . shooting star . . . signals from space . . . solar system . . . space station . . . speed of light . . . Star Trek . . . Star Wars . . . tracking station.

Entry Example

I prefer (soup) because . . . in my grocer's GALAXY of canned soups, (soup) is the brightest STAR for SKY-HIGH value at a price that's DOWN TO EARTH.

STOCK MARKET

account
acquisition
advance
assets
audit
bear
bid
Black Monday
block
blue chip
bond
boom
borrow
break
broker
bull
buy
capital
capitalize
cash
certificate
chart
clean up
closed-end
fund
collapse
collateral
commission
commodity
common
company
control
convert
corner

corporation
coupon
crash
credit
curb
deal
dealer
debit
debt-based
   assets
decline
deflation
depress
depression
dip
discount
dividend
downtrend
dump
earnings
equity
exchange
fall
figure
finance
firm
fiscal
fleece
float
floor
fluctuate
flurry
free fall
fundamental

analysis
funds
future
gilt-edge
global
   investing
go down
government
   security
hedge
high
hold
holdings
income
index
industrial
industry
inflation
interest
invest
investment
issue
junk bond
killing
lamb
lend
leverage
leveraged
   buy out
liability
limited
   partnership
liquidate
list

loan
loss
low
manipulate
margin
market
market maker
maturity
melon
merger
money market
  fund
monopoly
move up
municipal
mutual
mutual fund
negotiable
negotiate
note
obligation
offer
operator
option
order
panic
par
pay
payable
peg
penny stock
pink sheets
plum
plunge

point
pool
portfolio
preferred
premium
price
profit
promote
prospectus
prosperity
proxy
purchase
pyramid
quotation
quote
rally
real estate
  investment
  trust
redeem
redemption
reserves
retire
rise
risk
sale
seat
security
sell
share
shareholder
short
skyrocket
slump

specialist
speculate
speculator
split
spread
squeeze
stake
stock
stock exchange
stock market
stockholder
syndicate
takeover
technical
  analysis
technical
  indicators
ticker
tip
trade
transact
transaction
transfer
trend
turnover
underwrite
up trend
up tick
value
venture
volume
Wall Street
yield
zoom

Stock Market Phrases

Above par . . . annual report . . . balance sheet . . . bear market . . . below par . . . bid and asked . . . big board . . . blue-sky law . . . bottom dropped out . . . bucket shop . . . bull market . . . bulls and bears . . . buy low, sell high . . . capital gains . . . cats and dogs . . . caught short . . . close firm . . . common stock . . . corner the market . . . coupon clipper . . . declare a dividend . . . Dow Jones average . . . Dun & Bradstreet . . . fleece the lambs . . . float a loan . . . frozen assets . . . gilt-edge security . . . growth stock . . . heavy industry . . . hold for a rise . . . liquid assets . . . make a killing . . . net price . . . new high . . . new low . . . on the floor . . . open market . . . over the counter . . . paper profits . . . par value . . . preferred stock . . . profit and loss . . . puts and calls . . . sell short . . . sinking fund . . . stocks and bonds . . . stop-loss order . . . ticker tape . . . unlisted stock . . . ups and downs . . . watered stock . . . working capital.

Entry Example

I prefer to deal at (super market) because . . . a near CLOSING shopping FLURRY in this super MARKET never PANICS me, for its varied STOCK OFFERS me the widest OPTION of selection.

TAX

account
accountant
accrue
agent
amount
assess
assessment
assets
audit
balance
bank
benefit
bill
blank
calculate
capital
cash
casualty
charge
chart
check
city
claim
collect
collector
compute
contribution
credit
debt
declaration
declare
deduct
deductible
deduction

dependent
deposit
depreciate
direct
dividend
donation
due
earn
earned income
earnings
employer
estimate
evade
evasion
examine
exempt
exemption
expenses
federal
fee
FICA
figure
file
fill out
finance
fiscal
form
fund
gains
gross
gross income
high
household
income

increase
indirect
installment
interest
internal
  revenue
IRS
itemize
joint
levy
liability
liable
lien
liquidate
local
loophole
maintenance
net
net income
nontaxable
overpay
owe
pay
payment
penalize
penalty
percentage
profit
proof
raise
rapid refund
rate
rebate
receipt

receive	schedule	tax-deductible
record	separate	tax-exempt
reduce	share	tax-free
reduction	source	taxable
reform	spend	taxable income
refund	stamp	taxpayer
refundable	standard	toll
relief	deduction	treasury
repay	state	underpay
report	support	value
return	surtax	wages
revenue	table	withhold
salary	tariff	withholding tax
sales tax	tax	worth

Tax Phrases

After taxes . . . capital gains or losses . . . community property . . . excess profits . . . expense account . . . fair market value . . . figures don't lie . . . frozen assets . . . gainfully employed . . . head of household . . . hidden taxes . . . high cost of living . . . income tax . . . itemized deduction . . . joint return . . . no taxation without representation . . . nothing is certain but death and taxes . . . poll tax . . . profit and loss . . . social security . . . ways and means.

Entry Example

I bomb ugly bugs with (bug spray) because . . . after weak insecticides TAXED my patience, I found that (bug spray's) NET VALUE ends pest RETURNS—and no bug's EXEMPT!

Tax Ticklers

Deep in the heart of taxes . . . Do Eskimos pay a Pole Tax? . . . Nowadays, the earth revolves on its taxes.

Prosperity is something you feel, fold, and mail to the Internal Revenue Service.

TELEPHONE

accept
amplify
answer
answering
  machine
answering
  service
area code
automatic
bell
book
booth
bug
busy
buzz
buzzer
cable
call
cellular
central
circuit
classified
classify
click
code
collect
communicate
communication
conference
connect
connection
conversation
converse
cord

cordless
cradle
cut in
cut off
dial
dial tone
digit
direct
directory
disconnect
dispatch
dot
electronic
  fiber optics
exchange
extension
fax
file
flash
forward
hang up
headphone
hello
hook
hook up
index
information
instrument
intercom
key
line
listen
local
message

messenger
mobile
modem
Morse code
mouthpiece
number
numeral
operator
party
phone
phone book
pick up
plug in
pole
prepaid
receiver
relay
reply
ring
ring off
rollover
rotary
send
service
set
sign off
signal
spark
speak
station
switch
switchboard
system
talk

tap	toll	wireless
telegram	touch-tone	wiring
telegraph	transmission	wordsmith
telephone	transmit	
teletype	wire	

Telephone Phrases

Calling all cars . . . direct line . . . dots and dashes . . . get off the line . . . got your number . . . got your wires crossed . . . hold the wire . . . information, please . . . keep the wires hot . . . leave a message . . . let your fingers do the walking . . . live wire . . . night rates . . . off the hook . . . on the line . . . our answering machines have been talking . . . party line . . . person-to-person . . . pick up the phone . . . push-button dialing . . . reach out and touch . . . Red Book . . . ring the bell . . . station-to-station . . . take a call . . . ticker tape . . . toll charge . . . voice-activated . . . Western Union . . . who's calling? . . . wire tapping . . . wrong number . . . Yellow Pages.

Entry Example

When CALLING for this brand, I DIAL DIRECT to the best LINE available—the hottest NUMBER in any AREA!

Phoney Phun

In Iran, most telephone calls are Persian to Persian.

TENNIS

advantage
backhand
ball
championship
clay
court
defense
deuce
doubles
forehand
line
linesman

love
match
match point
net
offense
practice
racket
serving
set
shoes
singles
smash

tournament
victory
tennis
back court
game
mixed doubles
overhead
umpire
volley
Wimbledon

Tennis Phrases

Ball is in your court . . . don't feed me a line . . . feet of clay . . . he came home smashed . . . he/she is courting disaster . . . match maker . . . set in his/her way . . what a racket!

Illustration

They were a perfect MATCH. He fell in LOVE as soon as he began to COURT her.

TOOLS

adz	drill	joint
auger	drive	kit
awl	duct tape	knife
ax	dull	ladder
bar	edge	lathe
bind	fasten	level
bit	file	lever
blade	fix	leverage
block	force	line
blueprint	gadget	link
bolt	gauge	loosen
bore	gear	machine
brace	grind	magnet
build	grindstone	make
buzz saw	groove	mallet
caliper	hack	manual
carpenter	hacksaw	material
chain	hammer	mechanical
chisel	handle	mesh
chop	handy	metal
clamp	handyman	model
clip	hardware	mold
compass	hatchet	nail
construct	hinge	nipper
contraption	hoe	nut
contrivance	hold	pare
contrive	hole	penknife
crane	hook	pick
crowbar	implement	pile driver
cut	instrument	pin
cutter	iron	pincer
derrick	jack	pipe
design	jimmy	plane
device	join	pliers

plumb
point
pound
power
precise
precision
press
pressure
pry
pulley
pump
punch
rake
ram
rasp
ratchet
rip
ripsaw
rivet
rod
rule
sand
sandpaper

saw
scissors
scrape
screw
screwdriver
shape
sharp
sharpen
shears
shovel
sledge hammer
slice
slide rule
snip
solder
spade
spike
square
stake
stamp
staple
steel
stick

strap
strike
tack
tamp
tape
tighten
tongs
tool
tool box
torch
vise
washer
wedge
weld
wheel
wheelbarrow
whet
wire
wood
work
workshop
wrench

Tool Phrases

A chain is as strong as its weakest link . . . a straight line is the shortest distance between two points . . . an ax to grind . . . brace and bit . . . call a spade a spade . . . do it yourself . . . for want of a nail, a shoe was lost . . . hammer and tongs . . . Handy Andy . . . hard as nails . . . in the groove . . . loose nut . . . monkey wrench . . . Mr. Fix-it . . . nail down . . . no matter how thin you slice it, it's still baloney . . . nose to the grindstone . . . pick and shovel . . . power driven . . . shoulder to the wheel . . . spike a rumor . . . strike while the iron is hot . . . the right tool for the right job.

Entry Example

I trade with my local dealer because . . . he is a LEVEL-headed, SQUARE shooter who HANDLES only reliable merchandise—which AUGERS well for my confidence in him first, last and AWLways!

Carpenter's Slogan

Awl for one, and one for AWL!

TRAVEL AND TRANSPORTATION

18 wheeler
agent
airline
airplane
airport
airship
arrive
ATV
auto
automobile
aviation
baggage
barge
bicycle
boat
bridge
bus
byway
cab
camel
canal
canoe
car
caravan
cargo
carriage
carrier
carry
cart
chariot
coach
covered wagon
craft
cruise

cycle
debark
deliver
depart
destination
diesel
dog sled
drag
drive
electric
elephant
embark
engine
explore
express
expressway
fast
ferry
finish
flight
flight
  attendant
float
fly
freeway
freight
gasoline
gear
glide
glider
go
guide
hang glider
harness

haul
helicopter
highway
hitch
horse
horseback
horsepower
hot air balloon
itinerary
jaunt
jeep
jet
jitney
journey
lane
leave
liner
load
locomotive
luggage
machine
mail
manpower
map
messenger
mile
missile
mobile
motion
motor
motorcycle
mountain bike
move
moving van

mule
navigate
non-stop
nuclear
oil
omnibus
ox
ox-cart
pack-horse
passenger
path
payload
pedal
photos
pickup
pictures
pilot
pony express
power
propel
pull
push
raft
rail
railroad
railway
rapid transit
red eye
rickshaw
ride
river
road
rocket
roll
roller
route

run
rut
sail
schedule
scooter
sedan
semi
send
shay
ship
shipping
sky cap
sled
sleigh
slides
space shuttle
speed
stage coach
station
steam
steamboat
steamer
steer
stowaway
submarine
subway
suitcase
surface
taxi
ten speed
terminal
ticket
time-table
tire
toll
tow

track
tractor
tractor trailer
traction
traffic
trail
trailer
train
tram
transfer
transit
transport
transportation
travel
travelogue
trek
trip
trolley
truck
tugboat
turnpike
underground
van
vehicle
velocity
vessel
voyage
wagon
wagon train
waterway
wy
wheel
wing
zoom

Travel and Transportation Phrases

Beast of burden . . . bon voyage! . . . chart a course . . . coast-to-coast . . . from start to finish . . . get a move on . . . get the green light . . . give a lift . . . haul of fame . . . heavy load . . . highway and byway . . . horse and buggy . . . in a rut . . . Iron Horse . . . merrily we roll along . . . mile-a-minute . . . motive power . . . off the beaten path . . . oh what fun it is to ride in a one-horse open sleigh! . . . on board . . . on the go . . . one horse shay . . . put the cart before the horse . . . right of way . . . stop and go . . . take a ride . . . traffic jam . . . under way.

Entry Example

It pays to be courteous on subways and buses because . . . Courtesy is the OIL that smooths the TRACKS of daily TRAVEL, takes the friction out of crowded contacts, keeps all PASSENGERS in pleasant GEAR, and lets the WHEELS of regular RIDING ROLL along with smiling, not riling, results.

WEATHER

acclimate
air
almanac
atmosphere
autumn
balmy
barometer
beastly
below zero
blast
blizzard
blow
bluster
breeze
brisk
bulletin
calm
ceiling
centigrade
change
chart
chill
chinook wind
cirrus
clear
climate
clime
cloud
cloud burst
cold
condition
cool
cumulus
current

cycle
cyclone
damp
degree
deluge
dense
dew
disturbance
downpour
draft
drench
drizzle
dry
dust
elements
equator
erode
erosion
expose
exposure
fahrenheit
fair
fall
flash flood
fog
forecast
foretell
freeze
frigid
frost
gale
galoshes
gauge
glaze

greenhouse
guest
hail
heat
high
howler
humid
humidity
hurricane
ice
icicle
indoor
lightning
low
meteorologist
mist
moist
moisture
nature
observation
open air
outdoor
ozone
perspire
pleasant
polar
pole
pour
predict
pressure
puff
rain
rainbow
raincoat

rainfall
report
rubbers
sandstorm
Santa Ana
season
severe
shiver
shower
sizzle
sky
sleet
slush
smog
snow
snowfall
soak
spell
spring
squall
sticky
storm
storm warning

stuffy
summer
sun
sunny
sunshine
sweat
swelter
temperature
tempest
thaw
thermometer
thunder
thunderstorm
tornado
torrent
torrid
tropic
turbulence
twister
typhoon
umbrella
vane
vapor

velocity
ventilate
visibility
waft
warm
warmth
warn
weather
weathered
weather
  forecaster
weather vane
weatherproof
weatherwise
wet
whirlwind
wind
wind sock
winter
zephyr
zero
zone

Weather Phrases

Baby, it's cold outside . . . blow up a storm . . .
caught in the drift . . . change in the weather . . . cold
spell . . . cold wave . . . dog days . . . everybody talks
about the weather, but nobody does anything about it
. . . fair-weather friend . . . freezing point . . . greenhouse effect . . . heat wave . . . hot spell . . . in the
good old summertime . . . Indian Summer . . . is it hot
enough for you? . . . it's an ill wind that blows no
good . . . it's not the heat, it's the humidity . . . Jack
Frost . . . keep your weather eye open . . . liquid
sunshine . . . looks like rain . . . mackerel sky . . . nice

day for ducks . . . North Pole . . . overcast sky . . .
rain or shine . . . rain, rain go away . . . raining cats
and dogs . . . red sky at morning, sailors take warning
. . . South Pole . . . storm clouds . . . struck by lightning . . . torrid zone . . . trade wind . . . under the
weather . . . weather-beaten . . . weather bureau . . .
weather report . . . when it rains, it pours . . . when
it's springtime in the Rockies . . . Windy City . . .
winter wonderland.

Slogan

Drive like LIGHTNING and you'll crash like
THUNDER.

Weather Wit

Mexican weather report: "Chile today, hot tamale."

Meteorologist: A man who can look into a girl's
eyes and tell weather.

Weather forecaster: Someone with whom the
weather doesn't always agree.

WRITING

acceptance
advance
afterword
analogy
article
assignment
author
autobiography
banner
beat
biography
blue pencil
book
book club
broad sheet
bulletin
by-line
cable
campaign
caption
cartoon
censor
character
circulation
classified
climax
clipping
column
columnist
comics
composition
contract
copy
copyright

copywriter
copywriting
correspondent
cover
coverage
credit
critic
cub
cut
cut line
daily
dateline
deadline
dedication
desk
dispatch
dummy
edit
edition
editor
editorial
epigram
epilogue
excerpt
exclusive
extra
feature
fiction
file
filler
final
flashback
foreword
format

funnies
galley
ghost writer
graphic
grid
head
headline
house organ
index
insert
integrity
interview
issue
item
journal
journalism
journalist
kill
kill fee
layout
lead
libel
librarian
library
license
limerick
line
Linotype
make-up
masthead
mat
metaphor
morgue
nameplate

news	publish	side bar
news carrier	pump	signature
newsworthy	query	simile
nonfiction	query	slug
novel	quote	source
obituary	rag	space
op-ed pages	read	sports
page	reader	spread
paper	release	staff
paste up	report	stet
photographer	reporter	story
pick up	research	stringer
plate	review	style
play up	rewrite	submission
poem	rights	suppress
poll	royalty	syndicate
press	run	tabloid
pressman	scoop	timely
print	script	title
printer	serial rights	weekly
proof	series	write
proofread	sheet	write-up
publicity	short	writer's block

Writing Phrases

Advice to the lovelorn . . . all the news that's fit to print . . . bold face . . . capital letters . . . composing room . . . cover a story . . . cub reporter . . . fake a story . . . first draft . . . forgive us our press passes . . . Fourth Estate . . . freedom of the press . . . front page . . . members of the press . . . get the story . . . go to press . . . good copy . . . hold the press . . . human interest . . . in the public eye . . . inside story . . . lead story . . . make public . . . morning paper . . . press agent . . . press card . . . printer's ink . . . Pulitzer Prize . . . put the paper to sleep . . . roving report-

er . . . sob sister . . . sob story . . . special edition . . .
sport section . . . staff writer . . . star reporter . . .
stop the press . . . voice of the people . . . wire service
. . . yellow journalism.

Entry Example

I use (toothpaste) because . . . it won dental
NEWS HEADLINES with its anti-decay MAKE-UP
and helps me BEAT DAILY DEADLINES with its
EXTRA long-lasting FEATURES.

Writing Whimsey

In tomorrow's society, bookworms may become
tapeworms.

Author opening his mail: "We're gonna be rich!
Hollywood wants to pervert one of my novels."

If a biography is the story of a person's life, is an
autobiography the story of their car?

ZODIAC

almanac
Aquarius
Aries
ascendant
aspect
astral
astrologer
astrology
augur
augury
auspicious
beneficent
betoken
birth
birthday
bode
born
calendar
Cancer
Capricorn
cast
chance
chart
cipher
conjunction
cosmic
cryptic
date
decipher
destiny
detriment
disclose
divination
divine

divulge
dominant
Earth
fate
favor
favorable
force
forebode
forecast
foresee
foreshadow
forestall
fortunate
fortune
future
Gemini
guide
harbinger
heaven
herald
horoscope
house
ill-fated
indicate
influence
interpret
Jupiter
karma
karmic
Leo
Libra
luck
lucky
magic

Mars
Mercury
moon
mystery
mystic
natal
native
Neptune
occult
omen
ominous
oracle
period
Pisces
plane
planet
planetary
Pluto
portend
portent
power
predict
prediction
presage
prognosticate
promise
prophecy
prophet
prophetic
propitious
psychic
reveal
revelation
sage

Sagittarius	sphinx	unknown
Saturn	spirit	unlucky
Scorpio	square	unseen
seer	star	unveil
seeress	stargazer	Uranus
sibyl	stellar	Venus
sign	sun	vibrate
signify	symbol	vibration
sky	symbolic	Virgo
solar	system	vision
soothsayer	Taurus	warn
soothsaying	token	warning
sorcery	unfavorable	wizard
sphere	unfortunate	zodiac

Zodiac Phrases

Born under the sign . . . cast a horoscope . . . crystal ball . . . dominant factor . . . fortune teller . . . good omen . . . heavenly body . . . in the stars . . . lucky day . . . natal chart . . . natal day . . . out of this world . . . read the future . . . signs of the times . . . twelve signs of the Zodiac . . . what the stars say . . . what's your sign? . . . wheel of fortune.

Entry Example

I choose (light bulb) because . . . their CRYSTAL clarity and STELLAR performance REVEAL every SIGN of a bright FUTURE throughout my HOUSE.

INDEX

About the author . . .

Selma Glasser has crafted a successful career out of writing fillers, contest entries, light rhymes, and other short items for a variety of publications. Her work has appeared in *The New York Times, Reader's Digest, Good Housekeeping, Saturday Evening Post, Playboy, New Yorker, Harpers,* and the *Los Angeles Times,* to name a few. Additionally, Glasser is the author of five books and writes a syndicated column. She teaches several college writing courses, has authored a correspondence course on filler writing, and is in demand across the country as a seminar leader.

Her talents have led her to guest appearances on the "Today Show," "Hour Magazine," and numerous other TV programs. Selma's familiar voice has been heard on hundreds of radio shows. Glasser is listed in *Who's Who of American Women,* the *World's Who's Who of Women,* and *Who's Who Among Freelance Writers.*

Her contest entries—in which she frequently uses the analog formula—have won her such prizes as trips to Rome, Puerto Rico, and Paris. And Selma has dined as the guest of Sid Caesar and Englebert Humperdinck as a result of writing the most persuasive prose. Frank Sinatra even flew her to the Fontainebleau Hotel in Miami for his opening night performance. All this on top of winning a car, bundles of cash, and lots of merchandise. Selma Glasser is indeed a lady who practices what she teaches!

Readers of this book who have any questions of the usages of analogy in contest entries may obtain free advice by sending a stamped self-addressed envelope to the author:

> Selma A. Glasser
> 10240 Camarillo St., Suite 210
> Toluca Lake, CA 91602

Give the Gift of Writing Power to Your Friends and Colleagues!

ORDER FORM

YES, I want to help others discover the secret shortcut to power writing! Send _____ copies of *The Analogy Book of Related Words* at $12.95, plus $2 shipping per book. (Colorado residents please include $.91 state sales tax.) Canadian orders must be accompanied by a postal money order in U.S. funds. Allow 30 days for delivery.

$ ___ Check/MO enclosed • Charge my ☐ Visa ☐ MC

Name _____

Company _____

Address _____

City/State/Zip _____

Phone (____)_____

Card # _____ Expires_____

Signature _____

☐ Please send me information about your other books on writing. (See next page for selections.)

**Check your leading bookstore or
Call (719) 395-8659 for credit card orders.**

Communication Creativity
P. O. Box 909 • 425 Cedar Street
Buena Vista, CO 81211

See Over for Other Writing Books

MARKETING YOUR BOOKS: A Collection of Profit-Making Ideas for Authors and Publishers. Contains 13, in-depth chapters dealing with such topics as book club sales, premiums, radio interviews, and adding editorial "zingers" to increase book sales. Also a meaty section on how to write, design, and produce a sales-generating customer brochure. By Marilyn and Tom Ross, illustrated, indexed . . . trade paperback $9.95

THE COMPLETE GUIDE TO SELF-PUBLISHING: Everything You Need to Know to Write, Publish, Promote and Sell Your Own Book. An award-winning work, this is the most comprehensive manual available on the subject. A must for any author who wants to better understand book publishing and have personal impact on the sales and promotion of his or her own book. New revised and expanded edition. By Tom and Marilyn Ross, appendix, glossary, index, trade paperback . . . $16.95

NATIONAL SURVEY OF NEWSPAPER "OP-ED" PAGES. A one-of-a-kind directory of leading national newspapers. Cites needs, payment, who to contact, plus instructions on how best to market a message to this medium. A creative tool for authors, PR professionals, anyone seeking a forum to showcase ideas, industries, or individuals. Edited by Marilyn Ross . . . $19.95

HOW TO MAKE BIG PROFITS PUBLISHING CITY & REGIONAL BOOKS: A Guide for Entrepreneurs, Writers, and Publishers. Explores how to get a dynamite idea for an area book, do research, generate needed cash, make editorial and production decisions, and launch successful regional marketing campaigns. By Marilyn and Tom Ross . . . trade paperback $14.95

BOOK PROMOTION & MARKETING: Success Strategies to Increase Your Sales. A 6-hour cassette tape program and workbook offering the latest information on winning PR and sales strategies for authors, self-publishers and independent presses. Explores channels for distribution, free PR, direct mail campaigns, special sales, plus much more. By Marilyn and Tom Ross . . . $69.95

Please Include $2 Shipping per Book
(See *over* for ordering address)